Theo G. M. Sandfort, PhD
Jany Rademakers, PhD
Editors

Childhood Sexuality: Normal Sexual Behavior and Development

Childhood Sexuality: Normal Sexual Behavior and Development has been co-published simultaneously as *Journal of Psychology & Human Sexuality*, Volume 12, Numbers 1/2 2000.

Pre-publication REVIEWS, COMMENTARIES, EVALUATIONS . . .

Childhood Sexuality: Normal Sexual Behavior and Development

Childhood Sexuality: Normal Sexual Behavior and Development has been co-published simultaneously as *Journal of Psychology & Human Sexuality*, Volume 12, Numbers 1/2 2000.

The *Journal of Psychology & Human Sexuality* Monographic "Separates"

Below is a list of "separates," which in serials librarianship means a special issue simultaneously published as a special journal issue or double-issue *and* as a "separate" hardbound monograph. (This is a format which we also call a "DocuSerial.")

"Separates" are published because specialized libraries or professionals may wish to purchase a specific thematic issue by itself in a format which can be separately cataloged and shelved, as opposed to purchasing the journal on an on-going basis. Faculty members may also more easily consider a "separate" for classroom adoption.

"Separates" are carefully classified separately with the major book jobbers so that the journal tie-in can be noted on new book order slips to avoid duplicate purchasing.

You may wish to visit Haworth's website at . . .

http://www.HaworthPress.com

. . . to search our online catalog for complete tables of contents of these separates and related publications.

You may also call 1-800-HAWORTH (outside US/Canada: 607-722-5857), or Fax 1-800-895-0582 (outside US/Canada: 607-771-0012), or e-mail at:

getinfo@haworthpressinc.com

Childhood Sexuality: Normal Sexual Behavior and Development, edited by Theo G. M. Sandfort, PhD, and Jany Rademakers, PhD (Vol 12, No. 1/2, 2000). *"Important . . . Gives voice to children about their own 'normal' sexual curiosities and desires, and about their behavior and development." (Gunter Schmidt, PhD Professor, Department of Sex Research, University of Hamburg, Germany)*

Sexual Offender Treatment: Biopsychosocial Perspectives, edited by Eli Coleman, PhD, and Michael Miner, PhD (Vol. 11, No. 3, 2000). *"This guide delivers a diverse look at the complex and intriguing topic of normal child sexuality and the progress that is being made in this area of research."*

New International Directions in HIV Prevention for Gay and Bisexual Men, edited by Michael T. Wright, LICSW, B. R. Simon Rosser, PhD, MPH, and Onno de Zwart, MA (Vol. 10, No. 3/4, 1998). *"Performs a great service to HIV prevention research and health promotion. . . . It takes the words of gay and bisexual men seriously by locating men's sexual practice in their love relationships and casual sex encounters and examines their responses to HIV." (Susan Kippax, Associate Professor and Director, National Center in HIV Social Research, School of Behavioral Sciences, Macquarie University, New South Wales, Australia)*

Sexuality Education in Postsecondary and Professional Training Settings, edited by James W. Maddock (Vol. 9, No. 3/4, 1997). *"A diverse group of contributors–all experienced sexuality educators–offer summary information, critical commentary, thoughtful analysis, and projections of future trends in sexuality education in postsecondary settings. . . . The chapters present valuable resources, ranging from historical references to contemporary websites." (Adolescence)*

Sexual Coercion in Dating Relationships, edited by E. Sandra Byers and Lucia F. O'Sullivan (Vol. 8, No. 1/2, 1996). *"Tackles a big issue with the best tools presently available to social and health scientists. . . . Perhaps the most remarkable thing about these excellent chapters is the thread of optimism that remains despite the depressing topic. Each author. . . chips away at oppression and acknowledges the strength of women who have experienced sexual coercion while struggling to eliminate sexist assumptions that deny women sexual autonomy and pleasure." (Namoi B. McCormick, PhD, Professor, Department of Psychology, State University of New York at Plattsburgh)*

HIV/AIDS and Sexuality, edited by Michael W. Ross (Vol. 7, No. 1/2, 1995). *"An entire volume on the topic of HIV and sexuality, bringing together a number of essays and studies, which cover a wide range of relevant issues. It really is a relief to finally read some research and thoughts about sexual functioning and satisfaction in HIV-positive persons." (Associate of Lesbian and Gay Psychologists)*

Gender Dysphoria: Interdisciplinary Approaches in Clinical Management, edited by Walter O. Bockting and Eli Coleman (Vol. 5, No. 4, 1992). *"A useful modern summary of the State-of-the-art endocrine and psychiatric approach to this important problem." (Stephen B. Levine, MD, Clinical Professor of Psychiatry, School of Medicine, Case Western Reserve University; Co-Director, Center for Marital and Sexual Health)*

Sexual Transmission of HIV Infection: Risk Reduction, Trauma, and Adaptation, edited by Lena Nilsson Schönnesson, PhD (Vol. 5, No. 1/2, 1992). *"This is an essential title for understanding how AIDS and HIV are perceived and treated in modern America." (The Bookwatch)*

John Money: A Tribute, edited by Eli Coleman (Vol. 4, No. 2, 1991). *"Original, provacative, and breaks new ground." (Science Books & Films)*

Childhood Sexuality: Normal Sexual Behavior and Development

Theo G. M. Sandfort, PhD
Jany Rademakers, PhD
Editors

Childhood Sexuality: Normal Sexual Behavior and Development has been co-published simultaneously as *Journal of Psychology & Human Sexuality*, Volume 12, Numbers 1/2 2000.

The Haworth Press, Inc.
New York • London • Oxford

Childhood Sexuality: Normal Sexual Behavior and Development has been co-published simultaneously as *Journal of Psychology & Human Sexuality,* Volume 12, Numbers 1/2 2000.

The development, preparation, and publication of this work has been undertaken with great care. However, the publisher, employees, editors, and agents of The Haworth Press and all imprints of The Haworth Press, Inc., including The Haworth Medical Press® and Pharmaceutical Products Press®, are not responsible for any errors contained herein or for consequences that may ensue from use of materials or information contained in this work. Opinions expressed by the author(s) are not necessarily those of The Haworth Press, Inc.

Cover design by Thomas J. Mayshock Jr.

The Haworth Press, Inc., 10 Alice Street, Binghamton, NY 13904-1580 USA

Library of Congress Cataloging-in-Publication Data

Childhood sexuality : normal sexual behavior and development / Theo G.M. Sandfort, Jany Rademakers, editors.
     p. cm.
    "Co-published simultaneously as Journal of psychology & human sexuality, volume 12, numbers 1/2 2000"
    Includes bibliographical references and index.
    ISBN 0-7890-1198-0 (alk. paper)–ISBN 0-7890-1199-9 (alk. paper)
    1. Psychosexual development. 2. Children–Sexual behavior. I. Sandfort, Theo, 1953- II. Rademakers, Jany. III. Journal of psychology & human sexuality.
BF723.S4 C48 2000
306.7′083–dc21
                                                                              00-061353

Indexing, Abstracting & Website/Internet Coverage

This section provides you with a list of major indexing & abstracting services. That is to say, each service began covering this periodical during the year noted in the right column. Most Websites which are listed below have indicated that they will either post, disseminate, compile, archive, cite or alert their own Website users with research-based content from this work. (This list is as current as the copyright date of this publication.)

Abstracting, Website/Indexing Coverage .... Year When Coverage Began

- *BUBL Information Service, An Internet-based Information Service for the UK higher education community <URL:http://bubl.ac.uk/>* **1995**
- *Cambridge Scientific Abstracts* **1992**
- *CNPIEC Reference Guide: Chinese National Directory of Foreign Periodicals* **1995**
- *Educational Administration Abstracts (EAA)* **1995**
- *Family Studies Database (online and CD/ROM)* **1996**
- *Family Violence & Sexual Assault Bulletin* **1991**
- *FINDEX <www.publist.com>* **1999**
- *Gay & Lesbian Abstracts* **2000**
- *GenderWatch <www.slinfo.com>* **1999**
- *Higher Education Abstracts, providing the latest in research & theory in more than 140 major topics* **1991**
- *IBZ International Bibliography of Periodical Literature* **1996**
- *Index to Periodical Articles Related to Law* **1991**

(continued)

Special Bibliographic Notes related to special journal issues (separates) and indexing/abstracting:

- indexing/abstracting services in this list will also cover material in any "separate" that is co-published simultaneously with Haworth's special thematic journal issue or DocuSerial. Indexing/abstracting usually covers material at the article/chapter level.
- monographic co-editions are intended for either non-subscribers or libraries which intend to purchase a second copy for their circulating collections.
- monographic co-editions are reported to all jobbers/wholesalers/approval plans. The source journal is listed as the "series" to assist the prevention of duplicate purchasing in the same manner utilized for books-in-series.
- to facilitate user/access services all indexing/abstracting services are encouraged to utilize the co-indexing entry note indicated at the bottom of the first page of each article/chapter/contribution.
- this is intended to assist a library user of any reference tool (whether print, electronic, online, or CD-ROM) to locate the monographic version if the library has purchased this version but not a subscription to the source journal.
- individual articles/chapters in any Haworth publication are also available through the Haworth Document Delivery Service (HDDS).

ABOUT THE EDITORS

Theo Sandfort, PhD, is a social psychologist and Assistant Professor in the Department of Clinical Psychology at Utrecht University in the Netherlands. He also directs research in diversity, lifestyles, and health at the Netherlands Institute of Social Sexological Research (NISSO). In his doctoral research he studied the sexual experiences of children and adolescents (both consensual and non-consensual) with peers and adults, and the impact of these experiences on sexual functioning in later life. Other research areas he is involved with include gay and lesbian relationships, homosexuality and mental health, HIV/STD and sexual behavior, and sexual health policy.

Jany Rademakers, PhD, studied developmental and clinical psychology at Utrecht University in the Netherlands. From 1985 until 1992, she was Research Coordinator of Stimezo Nederland, the Dutch association of abortion clinics. In 1991, she wrote her thesis on the prevention of unwanted pregnancies by adolescents in the Netherlands. She has worked since 1992 at the Netherlands Institute of Social Sexological Research (NISSO) in Utrecht, where she is in charge of the research department called Sexuality Across the Life Cycle. Her main research themes are the sexual development and behavior of children and adolescents, and determinants of safe sex behavior.

Childhood Sexuality: Normal Sexual Behavior and Development

CONTENTS

Introduction

This special volume of the *Journal of Psychology & Human Sexuality* about child sexuality is an exceptional event.[1] Child sexuality is a rather neglected field in sex research. One might get a different impression, though, if one searches the scientific literature with 'child sexual development' as a search term. However, almost all references one will find deal either directly or indirectly with sexual abuse. There are very few papers about what one might call 'normal child sexual behavior.' It is hard to avoid the impression that the only way in which children figure in sexological research is as objects of sexual abuse. The child as a subject learning about sexuality and capable of experiencing sexual pleasures doesn't seem to exist in scholarly papers.

Why is there so little research into child sexuality? There are two related answers to this question. First of all, child sexuality is a very sensitive issue. If people, and parents in particular, are even willing to accept the idea that children have sexual feelings and desires, it is unlikely that they are willing to let their child participate in a study focussing on sexuality. The innocence of the child has to be protected and participation in research might injure that innocence. Children are supposed to develop their sexuality without any interference from outside. An unintended consequence of the discussions about sexual abuse might be that each interest in child sexuality, even that of researchers, is suspect.

The other answer is methodological. Regardless of its sensitive nature, child sexuality is hard to study. First of all, like in adults, sexual behavior in children is private behavior, which can only be observed by people who interact very frequently and intimately with the child. Children themselves are rather restricted sources to collect information about their sexuality, partly because their understanding of what sexuality is and also because of their capacity to conceive and

---

[Haworth co-indexing entry note]: "Introduction." Co-published simultaneously in *Journal of Psychology & Human Sexuality* (The Haworth Press, Inc.) Vol. 12, No. 1/2, 2000, pp. 1-3; and: *Childhood Sexuality: Normal Sexual Behavior and Development* (ed: Theo G. M. Sandfort, and Jany Rademakers) The Haworth Press, Inc., 2000, pp. 1-3. Single or multiple copies of this article are available for a fee from The Haworth Document Delivery Service [1-800-342-9678, 9:00 a.m. - 5:00 p.m. (EST). E-mail address: getinfo@haworthpressinc.com].

1

to express what they experience is developing, too. Furthermore, children may have developed a notion that this specific behavior has a special meaning to adults, and they might feel that it is not allowed to discuss these things. However, if one goes beyond the narrow definition of human sexuality in terms of desire, excitement and orgasm, and tries to study child sexuality in terms that are relevant to children themselves, important data might be collected. Methods and instruments to do so have to be developed and questions about the validity and reliability of these instruments have to be faced.

There is a practical need for information about child sexuality. The discoveries and discussions in the area of child sexual abuse already stressed this need. Since 'abnormal' sexual interest and behavior is regarded as a potential indication of abuse, it is important to find out what should be considered 'normal' and 'abnormal.' Valid information about child sexuality could also take away uncertainties in parents regarding their children's behavior. Even if we neglect or ignore sexuality in children, the child continues to learn about sexuality. Not being informed about child sexuality makes it difficult to respond to expressions of child sexuality and, if necessary, to support the child if there are problems.

This volume does not purposefully focus on sexual abuse. The papers in this volume all deal with what could be called 'normal' sexual behavior and development in children under age 12. The first three papers report on qualitative studies. Volbert, who studied what children in the ages from 2 to 6 know about sexuality, shows that different domains of sexual knowledge can be distinguished. Schuhrke studied longitudinally the process of body discovery in the same age group, in particular the interest of children in other people's genitals. Rademakers, Laan and Straver describe how, in their own words, boys and girls in the age of 8 to 9 years experience different kinds of physical intimacy. In their quantitative study, Meyer-Bahlburg, Dolezal and Sandberg tested in a community sample whether there is an association between childhood sexual behavior and externalizing behavior problems, as suggested by existing data. From a methodologcal perspective, O'Sullivan, Meyer-Bahlburg and Wasserman explored the responses of 7 to 13 year old boys and their mothers to completing an individual interview about their sexual behavior. In the last two articles, by Sandfort and Cohen-Kettenis and by Friedrich et al., data from observational studies are presented. These papers show the variety between children based on age and gender, but they also suggest the importance of the situation in which the child develops, both at the small scale of the family as well as the larger scale of the cultural climate of a country.

What the articles have in common is that they all try to deal in their own way with the possibilities and the difficulties of doing research on children's sexuality. Although not a state of the art, we hope that the articles in this special issue stimulate thought and discussion on the issue of child sexuality and promote further research in this rather unexplored field.

Theo G. M. Sandfort, PhD
Jany Rademakers, PhD

NOTE

1. Earlier versions of most of the papers in this volume have been presented at a symposium on child sexuality, which was held at the 22nd Annual Meeting of the International Academy of Sex Research in Provincetown, MA.

Sexual Knowledge of Preschool Children

Renate Volbert, PhD

ABSTRACT. In an investigation of sexual knowledge, 147 children between the ages of 2 and 6 were interviewed. While children of all ages had knowledge of gender identity, genital differences, and sexual body parts, they demonstrated little understanding of pregnancy, birth, and procreation, and revealed almost no information on adult sexual behavior. Age differences for all investigated areas of knowledge were found. There was definite development among the ages studied in knowledge of pregnancy and birth, but only a slight increase for the areas of procreation and adult sexual behavior. *[Article copies available for a fee from The Haworth Document Delivery Service: 1-800-342-9678. E-mail address: <getinfo@haworthpressinc.com> Website: <http://www.HaworthPress.com>]*

KEYWORDS. Sexual knowledge, early childhood, age differences, interview

INTRODUCTION

Due to growing concern over child sexual abuse, children's knowledge of sexuality has taken on increased importance. Age-inappropriate sexual knowledge is often regarded as an important indicator in substantiating alleged sexual abuse (Friedrich, 1993). Yet very little has actually been determined on what children know about sexuality.

Renate Volbert, Institut für Forensische Psychiatrie der FU Berlin, Limonenstr. 27, D-12203 Berlin, Germany.

[Haworth co-indexing entry note]: "Sexual Knowledge of Preschool Children." Volbert, Renate. Co-published simultaneously in *Journal of Psychology & Human Sexuality* (The Haworth Press, Inc.) Vol. 12, No. 1/2, 2000, pp. 5-26; and: *Childhood Sexuality: Normal Sexual Behavior and Development* (ed: Theo G. M. Sandfort, and Jany Rademakers) The Haworth Press, Inc., 2000, pp. 5-26. Single or multiple copies of this article are available for a fee from The Haworth Document Delivery Service [1-800-342-9678, 9:00 a.m. - 5:00 p.m. (EST). E-mail address: getinfo@haworthpressinc.com].

5

There is, moreover, no consensus as to what in fact constitutes age-appropriate sexual knowledge among children. Empirical investigations of children's knowledge of sexuality have examined the following aspects:

- Genital differences
- Gender identity/constancy
- Pregnancy (fertilization and intrauterine development)
- Birth
- Procreation
- Sexual activities of adults
- Sexual abuse

However, several limitations must be emphasized: most work has focused on the development of gender identity and children's understanding of pregnancy and birth, whereas only scant empirical research has been conducted on other aspects of child sexual knowledge. Only a few studies have explicitly investigated knowledge of adult sexual behavior, or children's understanding of sexual abuse. Not only has little empirical research been conducted in this field, but most available studies are also quite dated. Access to sexually explicit material–such as pornographic videos and magazines–has by now become much more widespread. As a result, patterns of acquiring sexual knowledge may well have changed to some degree, since those children whose access to sexually explicit material is potentially easier than in earlier generations, may acquire more extensive sexual knowledge. Child knowledge on sexuality furthermore differs among cultures (e.g., Currier, 1981; Goldman & Goldman, 1982); results of existing studies are therefore applicable only within a cultural context similar to that in which the investigation was conducted.

Knowledge of genital differences and gender identity. The most comprehensive research has been conducted in this area of knowledge (e.g., Bem, 1989; Bosinski, 1989; Goldman & Goldman, 1982; Slaby & Frey, 1975; Thompson & Bentler, 1971, 1973). These studies show a developmental progression in children's understanding of gender. By ages 2 to 3, children learn to identify themselves as either boys or girls, and shortly afterwards they are able to identify the sex of others. Young children define sex primarily on the basis of salient visual cues such as clothing and hair, but most of them are aware of genital differences (e.g., Gordon, Schroeder & Abrams, 1990). It appears definite, however, that a child's gender identity is well developed before he or she generally acquires proper appreciation of sex differences, and that gender identity clearly develops before gaining full understanding of the genital basis of sex differences. Under ordinary circumstances, gender identity is well established by the age of 3 to 4 (Rutter, 1980).

Bem (1989) found girls to have significantly more genital knowledge than do boys. Her female subjects had as much genital knowledge at age 3 as males had by age 5. In Bem's study, 58% of the girls and 15% of the boys, ages 3 to 5, provided a label for female genitalia, and 67% of the boys and 68% of the girls, for male genitalia. These results accord with Bosinski (1989), who also found significantly better genital knowledge among 4- to 7-year-old girls than among boys of the same age. Data by Moore and Kendall (1971) on 3- to 5-year-old children do not confirm better overall knowledge among girls, but verify that children in general are better equipped with labels for male than for female genitalia (see also Gordon et al., 1990; Victor, 1980). The least knowledge can be found among boys concerning female genitalia. Additional support for this pattern is provided by Fraley, Nelson, Wolf, and Lozoff (1991), who showed that young girls (1 to 4 years old) were less likely than boys to receive a label for their own genitalia by their mothers, whereas they were more likely than boys to receive a term for the genitalia of the opposite sex. Terms employed for the female genitalia–e.g., "bottom"–are often not distinctive or differentiated from terms given for the anus (Moore & Kendall, 1971). When questioned, children between 2 and 7 seldom indicate any sexual function for genitalia. If they do so, these responses are primarily related to pregnancy and birth, such as "You make babies with it" (Gordon et al., 1990).

Knowledge of pregnancy and birth. Various studies show that children 4 to 7 years old possess very basic knowledge of pregnancy, namely of intrauterine growth, but only very little knowledge of birth, and almost no accurate knowledge of conception (Bernstein & Cowan, 1975; Bosinski, 1989; Cohen & Parker, 1977; Frasch & Grüninger, 1975; Goldman & Goldman, 1982; Gordon et al., 1990; Grassel & Bosinski, 1983; Kreitler & Kreitler, 1966; Löwe, 1981; Moore & Kendall, 1971).

Bernstein and Cowan (1975) stress the relevance of cognitive concepts to the understanding of the *origins of babies*, namely causality and identity. They suggest that children's concepts concerning the origin of babies follow a developmental sequence and are embedded in a matrix of cognitive-structural variables. At level 1, children are preformist and do not see the need for a cause of a baby. At level 2, causes are assimilated from notions of people as manufacturers. At level 3, two or three main factors are isolated by children: either social, sexual, or biological. Children at level 4 begin to coordinate the variables in a system of physical causes, but fail to grasp genetic transmission. Children at level 5 are able to understand genetic transmission, but conceptualize it as additive rather than interactive. At level 6, children are finally able to provide sophisticated theories of how people get babies. The authors conclude that children actively construct their notions about babies. 'What is often taken as misinformation may largely be a product of their own assimilative processes at work on materials with too complex a structure for them to understand' (p. 90). Goldman and Goldman (1983) found similar forms of children's explanations, although not in a clear progression. They categorized children as geographers (the only explanation is that the baby is inside the mother), manufacturers (the baby is made outside and put inside the mother by non-sexual means), agriculturalists (the seed-in-the-soil-analogy is taken literally), reporters (who know the facts, but cannot explain them), miniaturists (who believe that the baby is fully formed in miniature in either the sperm or egg), and realists (who have a reasonably accurate theory of fertilization and fusion). The fact that many children recognize sexual roles quite late seems not due to inherent difficulties in the problems posed, since some children at the age of 7 not only knew the facts, but also provided adequate explanations (Goldman & Goldman, 1983). Other studies further show that most young children (3 to 6 years) either have no explanation when asked about the origin of babies (Bosinski, 1989; Moore & Kendall, 1971), or believe that the baby has always been inside the mother (Cohen & Parker, 1977). Kreitler and Kreitler (1966) found that the most common theory among 4- to 5-year-old children is that the baby is created in the mother's belly from the food she eats, but this finding was not replicated in other studies. The assumption that preschool children are able to understand gestation inside the mother is corroborated by the results of Bosinski (1989): out of 366 four- to seven-year-old children, 21% related that the baby grows from an egg inside the mother's belly.

Preschool children generally do not realize any causal relation between the father and the pregnancy. The father's function is primarily seen in helping the mother (Kreitler & Kreitler, 1966; Moore & Kendall, 1971). Goldman and Goldman (1982) constructed a biological-realism scale to assess children's reports about *the mother's and father's role in procreation*. They identified 3 levels of nonsexual, transitional sexual, and overtly sexual answers, with mainly nonsexual roles in procreation being perceived up to 11 years. Many younger children, however, knew some of the facts before, but did not think of procreation in sexual terms. Whereas, in the presexual and nonsexual stages of children's thinking, mothers are apparently regarded as performing active roles, children later tend to see them as passive recipients in the sexual act when compared with the father's more active part.

When regarding *theories of birth*, the most common answer among 4- to 7-year-old children in most studies refers to opening of the belly (Bosinski, 1989; Grassel & Bosinski, 1983; Kreitler & Kreitler, 1966; Moore & Kendall, 1971). It was only in a study by Cohen and Parker (1977) that most children stated that the baby left the mother from a special hole, which they called either "vagina" or "bottom" among children vague with terms. Moore and Kendall (1971) found that 20% of children agreed that the anus could be a possible exit. However, agreement might have occurred to some extent because children did not actually differentiate between anus and vulva. Goldman and Goldman (1983) found anus responses to be evident among 5- and 7-year-olds. The authors also showed that English-speaking children (from USA, Australia, and England) tended to provide realistic accounts of birth exit by 11 years, among Swedish children, the corresponding age was 9 years. More than one-third of the Swedish sample gave a realistic answer already at age 5.

Children have rarely been interviewed on their *knowledge of adult sexual behavior* independent of the reproduction process. The above-mentioned studies indicate that children around 9 begin to give notions about the sexual act when asked about procreation (although some children know about coitus before). In studies with preschool samples, some children demonstrated knowledge of sexual intercourse, but these responses were generally very vague. It is therefore questionable whether these children actually had detailed knowledge about it. In addition, studies have not yet investigated young children's knowledge of other forms of adult sexual behavior.

Janus and Bess (1976) asked children from the age of 5 onward to tell or write a composition about certain sexual topics. Kindergarten children indicated that kissing is what one does sexually with the opposite sex. Children from grades two and three were most concerned with hugging, kissing, and dancing with the opposite sex. In the fourth and fifth grades, the following themes were predominant: touching and its association with sex, bodily shapes and personal tastes, awareness of intimate sexual activity, and privacy with the opposite sex. Grade six children provided specific knowledge of intercourse and its possible consequences. There was an increasing awareness of sexual desires and drives in this age group.

In a retrospective study, Gebhard (1977) found that knowledge of coitus steadily increases from early childhood until near puberty, when there is a marked acceleration in learning: over half of each sex reported to have learned of coitus by the end of their tenth year, and about 5% of the sample remembered having known about coitus before age 7. All females indicated that they did not know about penile erection before age 8, and only 3% reported that they knew about it before age 10. Most girls learned about it between the ages of 12 and 15. Approximately a quarter of the boys knew about penile erection before age 8, but more than 50% of the males reported that they were unaware of erections up to age 10.

Knowledge of sexual abuse. Wurtele and Miller (1987) found that conceptualizations of sexual abuse, descriptions of abusers and victims, and perceptions of the consequences of an abusive incident differ between 5- to 7- and 10- to 12-year-old children. Whereas most of the younger children were unable to define the term "sexual abuse," half of the older children provided a fairly accurate description by implying sexual contact. Of the younger children, only 15% gave descriptions involving sexual touching. The young group was more likely to perceive a perpetrator as being their own age and as being a stranger, than was the older group. Approximately 25% of the older group believed that sexual abuse involves serious physical aggression.

Moderating variables. As mentioned above, Goldman and Goldman (1982) found quite definite *cross-national differences* in children's sexual knowledge; the authors assume that this is due to different sex-education programs. Gordon et al. (1990) showed that parents' reports of *sex education* were positively related to overall sexual knowledge and to most areas of the sexual knowledge of 2- to 7-year-old children, but not to knowledge of adult sexual behavior. This may may be due to the fact that parents who do provide sex education primarily discuss pregnancy and birth, and not intercourse (Finkelhor, 1984). Gordon et al. (1990) also found that *parents' attitudes to children's sexuality* were significantly correlated with some areas of child knowledge and with overall knowledge. Children from *lower socio-economic backgrounds* demonstrated less overall sexual knowledge. Mothers of these children also reported more restrictive attitudes toward sexuality and offered their children less sex education than those in middle and upper social classes (Gordon et al., 1990). Elias and Gebhard (1974) found social class- and gender-interaction, with boys from lower social classes demonstrating knowledge of sexual behavior at an earlier age than boys from upper classes. This contrasted with findings obtained on girls from upper social classes, who knew more about sexual behavior than girls from lower social classes. Parents' reports of their *children's sexual behavior* were found to be correlated with the children's knowledge of sexual body parts and to their overall sexual knowledge, but not with knowledge of adult sexual behavior (Gordon et al., 1990) (see Volbert & van der Zanden, 1996).

The purpose of the present investigation (Volbert & Homburg, 1996) was to obtain currently valid information on what young children, ages 2 to 6, know about sexuality. We were especially interested in how the developmental progression in children's sexual knowledge varied in different areas of sexuality.

METHOD

Sample. We recruited 147 children (63 girls and 84 boys) between the ages of 2 to 6, from preschools at three different locations, in cities with total populations of 3,500,000, 37,000, and 5,000. Children were recruited as followed: Kindergarten teachers distributed flyers describing the study to parents. The flyer contained information on the purpose (gathering data on the development of children's sexual knowledge) and the method of the investigation. Parents were asked to indicate their interest in participation by entering their name on the flyer and returning it to the kindergarten teacher. Interested parents were shown the materials used in the study before they signed their consent. About 40% of the approached parents allowed participation of their children in the present study. Parents generally explained their refusal to allow participation by stating that the child was too young to be confronted with the topic of sexuality. This was especially prevalent among the parents of 2-year-olds. Distribution of the questioned children throughout the age groups was as follows: 2 years: n = 12; 3 years: n = 34; 4 years: n = 40; 5 years: n = 37; 6 years: n = 24. Mean age for girls was 4.5 and for boys 4.6 years; girls and boys were even distributed among the age groups. The majority of parents demonstrated an average level of education.

Child interview. Children were individually interviewed in their kindergarten. Drawings were used to lead into a discussion on the above-stated areas of children's knowledge of sexuality, i.e., they covered the areas of genital differences, gender identity, sexual body parts and their functions, pregnancy, birth, procreation, and sexual behavior of adults. The drawings depicted clothed and unclothed children and adults, a clothed pregnant woman, a semi-clad woman during the delivery of her baby, a semi-clad couple kissing and hugging, an unclothed couple hugging in bed, and an unclothed girl touching the penis of a boy the same age. For the topic "Sexual interactions between adults and children," pictures were shown of ambiguous situations which could be interpreted as sexual activities, but also as neutral functions involving adults' care or bathing of children: e.g., an adult leaning over an unclothed child, and a woman touching an unclothed boy's penis. In each area of discussion, the interviewer began by posing open-ended questions (for example, "What is this a picture of?" or "How does a baby get out of the belly?") and proceeded to more structured questions if the child gave an incorrect answer or no response to the less structured question (e.g., "Is this a boy or a girl?" or "Does the baby come out of the bottom, the navel, or the [child's expression for the female genitalia]?" If the child still did not provide an answer, the interviewer proceeded to the next area of discussion. Incorrect responses were not corrected, and incomplete answers were not finished by the interviewer. If a child demonstrated no knowledge on intrauterine development, areas dealing with birth and procreation were not discussed. Although the general format of the interview was the same for all ages, the interviewer frequently omitted discussion of birth and procreation areas with the 2- and 3-year-old children who revealed a lack of understanding of intrauterine development.

Coding. For each area of knowledge the children's responses were scored in different categories which reflected their knowledge level about that area (see the tables for the different categories). Two raters scored a random sample of 36 interviews; the correlations between both raters ranged from .77 to 1.00, with almost all correlations exceeding .90.

RESULTS

No significant differences between boys and girls appeared among any of the knowledge areas. Likewise, no significant differences resulted among the various cities at which data were collected. Kruskal-Wallis One-way ANOVAs revealed, as expected, significant age differences in all areas of knowledge (see Tables 1 to 7). In detail, the interviewed children demonstrated the following knowledge in the areas investigated:

In the area of *genital differences*, all children with the exception of one 2-year-old child were able to identify the respective sex when shown the picture material. The majority of the 2-year-olds did not explain their classifications; among the 3- and 4-year-olds, explanations were generally based on cultural characteristics such as hair. The majority of the 5- and 6-year-olds provided genital-related explanations: which, however, usually followed only after the picture with unclothed children was shown (Table 1).

With respect to *gender identity*, one fourth of the 2-year-olds, approximately 85% of the 3-year-olds, almost all 4-year-olds, and all 5- and 6-year-olds correctly identified their own sex. Most children who were able to do so also provided an explanation for their assignment. Among the 2- to 4-year-olds, statements made by others (such as "Because my mother said so") was the most prevalent explanation. Five- and six-year-old children gave explanations based on cultural characteristics such as clothing or earrings, or on genital-related explanations. In none of the age groups did the majority of the children explain their own gender identity on the basis of genital differences (Table 2).

In the area of *sexual body parts*, all children with the exception of 6 (4%; ages 2 to 4) knew a term for either male or female genitalia, and the majority of all ages provided labels for both genitalia. Five children (3%; ages 2 to 4) did not know a label for the male genitalia and

TABLE 1. Knowledge of genital differences at different ages (percentage at each age)

	2 years (n = 12)	3 years (n = 34)	4 years (n = 40)	5 years (n = 37)	6 years (n = 24)	Total (n = 147)
No knowledge	8.3	–	–	–	–	0.7
Correct identification of either boys or girls	33.3	8.8	10.0	2.7	–	8.2
Correct identification of both sexes without explanation	25.0	17.6	7.5	2.7	–	8.8
Correct identification of both sexes, explanation based on cultural characteristics	16.7	32.4	37.5	37.8	33.3	34.0
Correct identification of both sexes, genital-related explanation	16.7	41.2	45.0	56.8	66.7	48.3

Kruskal-Wallis One-way ANOVA: Chi^2 = 20.48; DF = 4; p < .001
Mann-Whitney U (p < .05): 2 < all
3 to 4 < 6

14 children (10%; ages 2 to 5) knew no term for the female genitalia. These data substantiate the pattern from earlier findings that children up to the age of 6 more frequently know labels for the male than for the female sexual body parts (e.g., Bem, 1989). The majority of the children gave elimination as the function for genitalia and claimed there was no further purpose. A total of 13 children (9%; ages 2 to 6) stated a sexual function for some body part; in most cases, these responses were related to birth (n = 10; 7%). Three children (2%) indicated a sexual function for the penis, but were not able to describe it more precisely. Two children (3 and 6 years old) said for example: "Seed go to the woman through the thing," and "There are seed in

TABLE 2. Knowledge of gender identity at different ages (percentage at each age)

	2 years (n = 12)	3 years (n = 34)	4 years (n = 40)	5 years (n = 37)	6 years (n = 24)	Total (n = 147)
No knowledge	75.0	17.6	2.5	–	–	10.9
Correct identification of one's own sex without explanation	–	23.5	15.0	–	8.3	10.9
Identification and some explanation	25.0	50.0	57.5	48.6	25.0	45.6
Identification and explanation based on cultural characteristics	–	–	12.5	29.7	29.2	15.6
Identification and genital-based explanation	–	8.8	12.5	21.6	37.5	17.0

Kruskal-Wallis One-way ANOVA: $Chi^2 = 50.03$; DF = 4; $p < .001$
Mann-Whitney U ($p < .05$): 2 < all
3 < 4 to 6
4 < 5 to 6

there, so that you can have a baby." Neither, however, demonstrated any further understanding of this process (Table 3).

With regard to *pregnancy,* almost three-quarters of all children questioned showed at least a vague knowledge of intrauterine growth. This was true even for a third of the 2-year-olds and half the 3-year-olds; the majority of all ages, however, could not explain the process. A total of 15 children (10%; ages 3 to 6) referred to fertilization, and two of these children were able to describe the process. Only a few children made patently false statements such as "Mom buys her babies" (claimed by a girl 3 years old). Other responses such as "The baby is picked up at the hospital" reflected accurate observations, but demonstrated ignorance of the complex process being investigated (Table 4).

When questioned on *birth,* a total of nine children (6%) between 3 and 6 provided statements on the birth process, by normal delivery and

TABLE 3. Knowledge of sexual body parts at different ages (percentage at each age)

	2 years (n = 12)	3 years (n = 34)	4 years (n = 40)	5 years (n = 37)	6 years (n = 24)	Total (n = 147)
No knowledge	25.0	2.9	2.5	–	–	3.4
Receptive understanding of a label for male or female genitalia	–	2.9	–	–	–	0.7
Expressive knowledge of label for male or female genitalia	–	8.8	10.0	8.1	–	6.8
Expressive knowledge for label of male and female genitalia	75.0	76.5	82.5	81.1	83.3	80.3
Knowledge of labels for genitalia and knowledge of sexual function of any body part		8.8	5.0	10.8	16.7	8.8

Kruskal-Wallis One-way ANOVA: Chi^2 = 9.31; DF = 4; p = .05
Mann-Whitney U (p < .05):   2 < 5 to 6

by cesarean section. A response involving cesarean delivery was assessed as correct only if elaboration followed: e.g., "If the baby is too big, then they have to cut open the belly." This exclusion criterion was applied because a number of children had basically assumed an incision in the stomach as the most probable possibility for delivery. Half of the 6-year-olds, almost half of the 5-year-olds, and a small number of the younger children (including a 2-year-old) were able to name one of the possible modes of birth. An additional 32% of all children suggested vague knowledge of the birth canal: e.g. "The baby comes out at the bottom," such responses occurred in most cases, however, only after explicit prompting. When prompted, around a third of the questioned children confirmed that birth was possible through the anus or the navel. Almost the same number of children claimed that delivery through the vagina was impossible. The majority of the chil-

TABLE 4. Knowledge of pregnancy at different ages (percentage at each age)

	2 years (n = 12)	3 years (n = 34)	4 years (n = 40)	5 years (n = 37)	6 years (n = 24)	Total (n = 147)
No knowledge	66.7	52.9	22.5	2.7	–	24.5
Mention of intrauterine growth when explicitly prompted	16.7	23.5	25.0	18.9	4.2	19.0
Mention of intrauterine growth	16.7	17.6	42.5	64.9	50.0	41.5
Explanation of intrauterine growth	–	–	2.5	8.1	12.5	4.8
Mention of fertilization	–	5.9	7.5	5.4	33.3	10.2

Kruskal-Wallis One-way ANOVA: Chi^2 = 53.02; DF = 4; $p < .001$
Mann-Whitney U ($p < .05$): 2 to 3 < 4 to 6
4 < 5 to 6
5 < 6

dren age 4 and older demonstrated at least vague knowledge of birth (Table 5).

With respect to the topic of *procreation*, only one 6-year-old evidenced knowledge of coitus. One child in each of the age groups from 3 to 6 was able to imply some knowledge of the process of conception. For example, a girl 4 years old explained, "A man and a woman have to cuddle up together, then the seed go from the man to the woman." An additional 7% of the children (ages 3 to 6) made statements on fertilization, but had no knowledge of coitus. A total of 90% of all children had no relevant knowledge whatsoever within this area: this applied for all 2-year-olds, more than 90% of the 3- to 5-year-olds, and two-thirds of the 6-year-olds. Nine of the children (6%) knew of the existence of the ovum, and eight children (5%) had knowledge of sperm. But only two children (a boy and a girl, both 6) were able to describe fusion of sperm and ovum in any way: "Daddy's got little seeds that swim through his thing into the egg." The most frequent assumption was that the egg was always in the belly of the mother, and that it suddenly begins to grow, for example, after the mother eats a

TABLE 5. Knowledge of birth at different ages (percentage at each age)

	2 years (n = 12)	3 years (n = 34)	4 years (n = 40)	5 years (n = 37)	6 years (n = 24)	Total (n = 147)
No knowledge	83.3	67.6	35.0	10.8	12.5	12.5
Mention of birth canal when explicitly prompted	8.3	11.8	37.5	32.4	12.5	23.8
Spontaneous mention of birth canal	–	11.8	10.0	5.4	8.3	8.2
Explanation of birth either by normal or cesarean means	8.3	5.9	15.0	43.2	50.0	25.2
Explanation of birth by normal and by cesarean means	–	2.9	2.5	8.1	16.7	6.1

Kruskal-Wallis One-way ANOVA: Chi^2 = 44.84; DF = 4; $p < .001$
Mann-Whitney U ($p < .05$):   2 to 3 < 4 to 6
                                4 < 5 to 6

great amount of food. In answer to the question of what a mother had to do if she wanted a baby, the children most frequently cited such measures as "get married" or "go to the hospital." Five children (3%) claimed that the mother would have to like the father very much, or cuddle and smooch with him. One girl, 6, pointed out that the woman would not be allowed to take a pill any more if she wanted a baby; another girl, 5, said that the woman would first have to bleed. When asked what the father would have to do to have a baby, 15% of the children explained that a father could not have a baby. Four additional children (3%) stated that the father didn't have to do anything at all. Approximately a fourth of the children mentioned social responsibilities of the father: especially, that he would have to earn the money (Table 6).

Questions on the subject *sexual behavior of adults* were intended to determine knowledge of sexuality independent of reproductive processes. None of the children up to age 5 demonstrated any knowledge

TABLE 6. Knowledge of procreation at different ages (percentage at each age)

	2 years (n = 12)	3 years (n = 34)	4 years (n = 40)	5 years (n = 37)	6 years (n = 24)	Total (n = 147)
No knowledge	100	94.1	92.5	94.6	66.7	89.8
Mention of fertilization	–	2.9	5.0	–	16.7	4.8
Description of fertilization	–	–	–	2.7	8.3	2.0
Mention of coitus	–	2.9	2.5	2.7	4.2	2.7
Description of coitus	–	–	–	–	4.2	0.7

Kruskal-Wallis One-way ANOVA: Chi^2 = 15.59; DF = 4; $p < .01$
Mann-Whitney U ($p < .05$):   2 to 5 < 6

of explicit sexual behavior. Three 5- and 6-year-old children (2%) provided descriptions of sexual actions. The farthest-ranging statement was given by a 6-year-old boy: "He goes with his thing to the wee-wee. Well, then they kiss, and the woman licks the man on his thing." This boy spontaneously added that he had once seen such an episode on a video cassette; he had no knowledge at all of the process of procreation. Five 5- and 6-year-old children (3%) revealed some knowledge of sexual behavior, but the responses again were related to the reproduction process: for example, "They make a baby with seed." Most of the responses, however, implied descriptions of cuddling, kissing, etc. (74%). Seventeen percent of the answers (from one-third of the 2-year-olds, one-fourth of the 3-year-olds, and 5% of each group from ages 4 to 6) did not even refer to such activities as cuddling and kissing. Four children (3%) (4 to 6) knew vulgar designations for sexual intercourse, but could not furnish further explanation of these terms (Table 7).

Sexual activities among children. When shown a picture in which a girl is touching a boy's penis, the majority of the children gave simple descriptions of the pictorial matter: e.g., "pointing to his thing," or "touching his thing." Fourteen children (13%) made statements which indicated forbiddance or their own rejection of sexual actions: e.g., "He mustn't do that. He'll get sick when he touches her wee-

TABLE 7. Knowledge of adult sexual behavior at different ages (percentage at each age)

	2 years (n = 12)	3 years (n = 34)	4 years (n = 40)	5 years (n = 37)	6 years (n = 24)	Total (n = 147)
No knowledge	33.3	23.5	5.0	5.4	4.2	11.6
Mention of kissing, cuddling, etc.	66.7	67.6	82.5	75.7	66.7	73.5
Mention of explicit sexual behavior	–	8.8	12.5	16.2	20.8	12.9
Description of explicit sexual behavior	–	–	–	2.7	8.3	2.0

Kruskal-Wallis One-way ANOVA: Chi^2 = 16.35; DF = 4; p < .01
Mann-Whitney U (p < .05):   2 to 3 < 4 to 6

wee," or "That girl's a piggy because she touches his thing." Two children made statements which went beyond the content of the picture. One girl, 5, reported sexual interaction with her brother, and another girl, 4, said, "My daddy also didn't like it when I touched his thing."

Sexual interactions between adults and children. When shown the picture of an adult bending over an unclothed child, most of the children described parental care activities such as diapering or applying cream. Only two of the children explicitly mentioned genital contacts: "The doctor has to touch my thing," or "Daddy laughs and grabs him on the winkie–that tickles." When shown a picture in which a woman touches a boy and the boy himself touches his penis, approximately half of the children (47%) claimed that the scene represented the mother's care for the genitals of the boy: washing, inspecting, pulling back the foreskin, applying cream, and helping during urination. Four children (3%) (two 3- and two 4-year olds) described actions not characterized by the intention to care for or clean the pictured boy: "Mommy tickles his thing and she likes to do it, too." And "Mommy's playing around with his thing." Although the picture shows two persons, 28 of the questioned children (20%) described actions by the pictured child alone: "The boy is playing around with his thing." Ten of the children (7%) pointed out that such actions were forbidden: ". . . because you'll get sick that way . . ." or ". . . because Mommy'll get mad. . . ." One boy explained that such behavior was forbidden because they could lead to loss of the genitals: "You shouldn't play with your thing, else it'll fall off and the boy will have a wee-wee instead."

DISCUSSION

The present study revealed the following developmental course of knowledge in the investigated areas:

2 years: Children correctly identify the sex of others, without being able to explain the differences
Children use colloquial terms to denote genitalia
3 years: Children explain gender identity on the basis of cultural characteristics
4 years: Children have a vague understanding of intrauterine growth
Children have a very vague knowledge of the birth canal
5 years: Children explain gender identity on the basis of genital differences
6 years: Children have knowledge of normal or cesarean parturition

The extent of knowledge of sexuality encountered here is very similar to that found in a relatively recent study by Gordon et al. (1990). The findings correspond on the whole to those described over the past three decades. One cannot therefore conclude that substantial changes have taken place during this period in the acquisition of sexual knowledge among preschoolers. Despite presently more readily available access to sexually explicit material, the children in the age group studied demonstrated practically no knowledge of the sexual behavior of adults. Now, as in years before, the great majority of the children in the age groups investigated apparently obtain initial sexual knowledge on the reproduction process, and gradually accumulate information on coitus and the sexual behavior of adults in this manner.

Important changes have taken place in comparison with the situation depicted in investigations conducted many years ago. In earlier studies (e.g., Conn, 1947), preschool children did not even mention the mother's role in the arrival of the baby, and the concept of the birth process was completely foreign to children of these ages. Conn concluded at that time that it was inconceivable to preschool children that the baby could be inside the mother. He reported beginning awareness of the mother's role around age 8. Accordingly, children around 9 years of age were supposed to think about various body apertures through which the baby could conceivably leave the mother. The typical 10- to 12-year-old was found to believe that the baby was in the mother's stomach and required surgical removal. Out of 100 children between 4 and 11 years whom Conn interviewed, only 6 were aware that some form of genital contact occurred between the sexes; half of them appeared to be puzzled or in doubt as to the purpose of genital contact or penetration. Bosinski (1989), as well as Grassel and Bosinski (1983), emphasize that erroneous information–such as stories about the stork etc.–can primarily be found in older studies (e.g., Brückner, 1968), in which such accounts involved up to 60% of children interviewed. Retrospective research likewise shows that the primary years for learning of pregnancy in older samples were those from 8 to 12, with the mode being 10. In a more recent sample, over half of the children knew of pregnancy before age 7, with the mode for boys being 6 and for girls, 5 (Gebhard, 1977). Unlike the actual sexual behavior of preschool children (e.g., Gordon & Schroeder, 1995; Volbert & van der Zanden, 1996), their sexual knowledge appears to be more extensively influenced by epochal changes.

In the age groups studied in the present investigation, most knowledge existed, as expected, in areas in which children were able to relate to their own immediate experience. This knowledge primarily involved gender identity and genital differences. Most of the 2-year-olds were already able to correctly identify the sex of represented persons. The augmentation of knowledge observed as the age of interviewed children increased primarily entailed the quality of explanations for the perception of sexual identity. Whereas most of the youngest children perceived "boy" and "girl" merely as labels, without understanding of the associated classification (cf. Maccoby, 1980; Thompson, 1975), 3-year-olds can provide explanations, initially related only to cultural characteristics (clothing, hair, etc.). This is apparently the case despite the fact that children at this age are already aware of genital differences. Even among 5- and 6-year-olds, explanations based on cultural characteristics were prevalent. If such differences were no longer apparent on the drawings shown, the children pointed out the different sexual body parts. Carey (1985) argues that-although gender identity is in fact highly significant for children–children consider it exclusively in its social significance, and not in terms of a fundamental biological category. According to Carey, biological basis begins to play a greater role when the child learns to theorize within the context of intuitive biology during the course of his or her first ten years of life. On the other hand, literal answering of the posed questions (e.g., "How do you know if someone is a boy or a girl?") underlines the significance of cultural characteristics: the child, after all, actually decides in the course of daily life on the basis of such characteristics. Accordingly, assignment of a person to one sex or the other on the basis of perception of his or her genitals most probably represents the exception in this context. With regard to the topics of pregnancy and birth, the majority of the children above the age of four demonstrated partial knowledge. Here as well, areas are involved in which many children can relate to immediate experience: e.g., encounters with pregnant women, pregnancy among acquaintances and relatives, etc. Only 10%, however, had specific notions concerning fertilization and coitus. Knowledge of adult sexual behavior was also very rare among the children in this study.

Carey (1985; 1988) describes the acquisition of knowledge not merely as the accumulation of facts, but as a process of restructuring of intuitive theories and has investigated these phenomena using examples from intuitive biology. She argues that the understanding of various areas of phenomena may be reduced to a small number of essential principles of explanation. Children begin with a very few intuitive theories and undergo a development characterized by the reorganization of their knowledge which is caused by modifications of these theories. Carey describes that children four to seven years old explain biological functions not from a biological standpoint, but within the context of an intuitive theory of behavior which explains behavior in terms of wants, beliefs and social conventions which Carey calls "naive psychology." It is only around 9 or 10 that the comprehensive role of intuitive behavioral theory is superseded by that of intuitive biology.

Carey's interpretation here accords with the observed phenomenon that preschool children–although they possess vague knowledge of intrauterine growth–explain the arrival of babies not from a biological standpoint, but in terms of the goals and the social behavior of parents (getting married, going to the hospital, liking each other, no longer taking a pill, and the like). A number of older children, to be sure, are able to state the significance of ovum and sperm: but without understanding of the physiological mechanisms. According to Carey, these processes represent a transition phase in which older children are already able to imagine inner bodily processes, but–like younger children-develop concepts of them in terms of human behavior.

On the basis of Carey's assumptions, it can be expected of children only after they reach ages of around 9 to 10 that they will be able to clearly differentiate between the level of the behavior of their parents and the level of the biological processes concerned. The studies referred to above on the knowledge of older children on reproduction processes support this hypothesis. Carey points out that children actively construct theories on the origin of babies, in accordance with their intuitive framework of theory, rather than merely reproducing received information. On the other hand, investigations comparing findings in different countries (Goldman & Goldman, 1982) call attention to the fact that the nature of information offered significantly influences the development of knowledge in this area.

Whereas the understanding of reproduction processes may depend on the nature of existing intuitive theories, knowledge of adult sexual behavior can principally be obtained independently of this aspect–e.g., gained by observation. Results of the present study suggest, however, that it is only in very exceptional cases that information about sexual behavior is obtained independently of sexual education covering the processes of reproduction. It may be assumed that the various means of attaining sexual knowledge exert an influence on the development of sexual concepts among children. The present study, however, cannot offer further insights in support of this assumption.

It must be pointed out that this study–on the basis of its sample size alone–is not representative. It is also significant that a large share of the parents approached refused to allow their children to be interviewed. There is no information on the differences between parents who allowed their children to be interviewed and parents who refused such permission. A further difficulty is the fact that children under certain conditions may well possess more sexual knowledge than they reveal during the interviews. This possibility is especially great among the older of the questioned children, since embarrassment with respect to sexuality has already become more pronounced at their ages (cf. Rosenfeld et al., 1984; see also Gordon et al., 1990). It would therefore prove valuable to supplement the present interview data by conducting, for example, a survey among kindergarten teachers on the sexual knowledge of children.

REFERENCES

Bem, S.L. (1989). Genital knowledge and gender constancy in preschool children. *Child Development, 60*, 649-662.

Bernstein, A.C., & Cowan, P.A. (1975). Children's concepts of how people get babies. *Child Development, 46*, 77-91.

Bosinski, H. (1989). Zum aktuellen Stand der Geschlechtserziehung im Vorschulalter. *Ärztliche Jugendkunde, 80*, 290-297.

Brückner, H. (1968). *Das Sexualwissen unserer Jugend*. Berlin: Deutscher Verlag der Wissenschaften.

Carey, S. (1985). *Conceptual change in childhood*. Cambridge: MIT Press.

Carey, S. (1988). Conceptual differences between children and adults. *Mind and Language, 3*, 167-181.

Cohen, B., & Parker, S. (1977). Sex information among nursery-school children. In E.K. Oremland & J.D. Oremland (Eds.), *The sexual and gender development of young children: The role of the educator* (pp. 181-190). Cambridge: Ballinger Publishing Company.

Conn, J.H. (1947). Children's awareness of the origins of babies. *Journal of Child Psychiatry, 1*, 140-176.

Currier, R.L. (1981). Juvenile sexuality in global perspective. In L.L. Constantine & F.M. Martinson (Eds.), *Children and sex. New findings, new perspectives* (pp. 9-19). Boston: Little, Brown and Company.

Elias, J., & Gebhard, P.H. (1974), Sexuality and sexual learning in childhood. In R. Rogers (Ed.), *Sexual education–rationale and reaction* (pp. 143-154). London: Cambridge University Press.

Finkelhor, D. (1984). *Child sexual abuse. New theory and research*. New York: The Free Press.

Fraley, M.C., Nelson, E.C., Wolf, A.W., & Lozoff, B. (1991). Early genital naming. *Developmental and Behavioral Pediatrics, 12*, 301-305.

Frasch, H., & Grüninger, W. (1975). Das Sexualwissen von Schulanfängern–Ein empirischer Beitrag zur Sexualpädogogik. *Medien und Sexualpädagogik, 3*, 1-5.

Friedrich, W.N. (1993). Sexual victimization and sexual behavior in children: A review of recent literature. *Child Abuse and Neglect, 17*, 69-66.

Gebhard, P.H. (1977). The acquisition of basic sex information. *Journal of Sex Research, 13*, 148-169.

Goldman, R., & Goldman, J. (1982). *Children's sexual thinking*. London: Routledge and Kegan Paul.

Goldman, R., & Goldman, J. (1983). Children's perceptions of sex differences in babies and adolescents: A cross-national study. *Archives of Sexual Behavior, 12*, 277-294.

Gordon, B.N., & Schroeder, C.S. (1995). *Sexuality. A developmental approach to problems*. New York: Plenum Press.

Gordon, B.N., Schroeder, C.S., & Abrams, M. (1990). Age and social-class differences in children's knowledge of sexuality. *Journal of Clinical Child Psychology, 19,* 33-43.

Grassel, H., & Bosinski, H. (1983). Sexualwissen und Geschlechterrollen-Vorstellungen bei Vorschulkindern. *Ärztliche Jugendkunde, 74,* 110-120.

Janus, S.S., & Bess, B.E. (1976). Latency: Fact or fiction? *The American Journal of Psychoanalysis, 36,* 339-346.

Kreitler, H., & Kreitler, S. (1966). Children's concepts of sexuality and birth. *Child Development, 37,* 363-378.

Löwe, B. (1981). Das sexualkundliche Vorwissen von Schülern der Eingangsstufe der Grundschule–eine Pilotstudie an nordbadischen Grundschülern. In N. Kluge (Hrsg.), *Sexualpädagogische Forschung* (S. 59-88). Paderborn; Schöningh.

Maccoby, E.E. (1980). *Social development.* New York: Harcourt, Bace, Jovanovich.

Moore, J.E., & Kendall, D.C. (1971). Children's concepts of reproduction. *Journal of Sex Research, 7,* 42-61.

Rosenfeld, A., Siegel-Gorelick, B., Haavik, D., Duryea, M., Wenegrat, A., Martin, J., & Bailey, R. (1984). Parental perceptions of children's modesty: A cross-sectional survey of ages two to ten years. *Psychiatry, 47,* 351-365.

Rutter, M. (1980). Psychosexual development. In M. Rutter (Ed.), *Scientific foundations of developmental psychiatry* (pp. 322-339). London: Heinemann Medical Book Ltd.

Slaby, R.G., & Frey, K. S. (1975). Development of gender constancy and selective attention to same-sex models. *Child Development, 46,* 849-856.

Thompson, S.K. (1975). Gender labels and early sex-role development. *Child Development, 46,* 339-347.

Thompson, S.K., & Bentler, P.M. (1971). The priority of cues in sex discrimination by children and adults. *Developmental Psychology, 5,* 181-185.

Thompson, S.K., & Bentler, P.M. (1973). A developmental study of gender constancy and parent preference. *Archives of Sexual Behavior, 2,* 379-385.

Victor, J.S. (1980). *Human sexuality: A social psychological approach.* Englewood Cliffs: Prentice-Hall.

Volbert, R., & Homburg, A. (1996). Was wissen 2–bis 6jährige Kinder über Sexualität? *Zeitschrift für Entwicklungspsychologie und Pädagogische Psychologie, 28,* 210-227.

Volbert, R., & van der Zanden, R. (1996). Sexual knowledge and behavior of children up to 12 years–what is age-appropriate? In G. Davies, S. Lloyd-Bostock, M. McMurren & C. Wilson (Eds.), *Psychology, law, and criminal justice. International developments in research and practice* (pp. 198-215). Berlin: de Gruyter.

Wurtele, S.K., & Miller, C.L. (1987). Children's conceptions of sexual abuse. *Journal of Clinical Child Psychology, 16,* 184-191.

Young Children's Curiosity About Other People's Genitals

Bettina Schuhrke, PhD

ABSTRACT. When children can satisfy their sexual curiosity and even when they are hindered in doing so, they learn something about specific aspects of sexuality, e.g., they construct a mental representation of their bodies and those of other people, including the sexual organs. An in-depth exploratory study on the process of body discovery has been conducted on 26 German children. In this article results are reported on children's interest in other people's genitals: their behavior, aspects of the situations in which the interest becomes manifest, and changes in interest from the second to the sixth year of life. Methods of data collection were observation by parents over the course of the second year of life and interviews with mothers at the beginning of the third and in the sixth year of life. *[Article copies available for a fee from The Haworth Document Delivery Service: 1-800-342-9678. E-mail address: <getinfo@haworthpressinc.com> Website: <http://www.HaworthPress.com>]*

KEYWORDS. Sexuality, body discovery, body representation, early childhood, parental observation, interview

INTRODUCTION

The curiosity of little children about the sexual characteristics of their own bodies and those of other people can be seen as an important

Bettina Schuhrke, Universitaet Mainz, Institut fuer Soziologie, Abt. fuer Familien Für Schung, 55099 Mainz, Institut für Soziologie, Abteilung für Familienforschung, Johannes-Gutenberg-Universität Mainz, 55099 Mainz, Germany.

[Haworth co-indexing entry note]: "Young Children's Curiosity About Other People's Genitals." Schuhrke, Bettina. Co-published simultaneously in *Journal of Psychology & Human Sexuality* (The Haworth Press, Inc.) Vol. 12, No. 1/2, 2000, pp. 27-48; and: *Childhood Sexuality: Normal Sexual Behavior and Development* (ed: Theo G. M. Sandfort, and Jany Rademakers) The Haworth Press, Inc., 2000, pp. 27-48. Single or multiple copies of this article are available for a fee from The Haworth Document Delivery Service [1-800-342-9678, 9:00 a.m. - 5:00 p.m. (EST). E-mail address: getinfo@haworthpressinc.com].

part of their sexual development. If we talk about curiosity, we at the same time address a motivational force, directed to explore the unknown, and the motivated behavior and its target objects.

To characterize a person as an individual sexual being at a certain point of his or her life time, one would have to elaborate on a number of different aspects of his or her sexuality (Schuhrke, 1991). Important aspects are the repertoire of sexual behavior of a person, the kind of cognitive and emotional representation of bodily experiences, the amount of intimacy and feeling a person can tolerate, characteristics of the persons an individual is sexually oriented to, the organization of his or her sexual role, identity, and script. In situations in which children can satisfy their sexual curiosity and indeed, even in situations in which they are hindered in doing so, they learn something about these specific aspects of sexuality. In the following, the most important gains will be discussed which children make in respect to these aspects when they explore their own bodies and those of other people.

First of all, exploration helps children to construe a body representation for both sexes. There are different strains of research on the representation of the body: the oldest one probably being the neurological (see Kolb, 1975; Poeck and Orgass, 1964), followed by the psychoanalytical (see Lemche, 1993; Schilder, 1950) and still later the psychological (e.g., Fisher and Cleveland, 1968). Based on this literature, one can assume that a process of body discovery takes place in children, which is characterized mainly by children becoming aware of their bodies as being part of themselves, and then beginning to represent it mentally. Such a representation changes constantly just as the body constantly changes throughout life. However, the earliest experiences are probably the most fundamental. At the beginning, it may just be the formation of a physiological body scheme, which the child is not necessarily conscious of, but which at the same time indicates the positions of certain organs in relation to each other, and makes possible the coordination of posture and movement (Head and Holmes, 1911/12). Later on, higher levels of representation are added which are more or less accessible to consciousness. Shontz (1974), for example, distinguishes on higher levels a "body self" and connected "body values," "body fantasies," such as the general impression of one's own body as attractive or efficient, and "body concepts" which may be relatively independent of direct experiences, for example they may be acquired by books.

The individual body parts take on increased meaning, depending on what their functions are, which sensory channels supply which kind of information to the representation (optic, kinaesthetic, tactile, olfactory), how they are evaluated and dealt with by significant others or the surrounding culture, the construction of analogies and metaphors in language. In addition, there are direct exchange processes between the body representations of individuals. Children pick up something about the way other people evaluate their own bodies and how they handle them and integrate this information into their own body representations (see Fisher, 1970; Schilder, 1950).

Children learn about the sexual organs in the general process of body discovery. However, developing a representation of the sexual organs, the child has to come to terms with some peculiarities of the socialization process. On the one hand, the genitals are the origin of strong pleasurable sensations when children play with themselves or during social interactions (e.g., diaper change), on the other hand, children are generally not allowed to relate to these parts by touching, looking, or speaking. Fisher states: " . . . although parents are isolating the genitals, they are transmitting expectations of future ability to perform traditional sex roles skillfully and vigorously. Concepts and ideas phrased in genital images are covertly infused while conscious recognition of such images is discouraged" (1989, p. 33).

Nowadays close physical contact with parents is recognized as important for the development of small children. However, close and especially nude physical contact probably directs children's attention to their bodies and those of other people and promotes children's sexual interest. Comparisons of institutionalized children with children living with families (Provence and Lipton, 1962; Spitz and Wolf, 1949) underline the importance of stimulation by a primary care-taker for children's genital play, but in these studies it is impossible to separate the physical component from the general amount of stimulation such a person provides for a child. In a study of Lewis and Janda (1988) of 210 students, exposure to nudity in childhood and sleeping in the parental bed is correlated with sexual activity, feeling comfortable with physical contact and affection, and self-esteem. Friedrich, Grambsch, Broughton, Kuiper, and Beilke (1991) report higher levels of sexual activity in children who are confronted with higher levels of nudity in their families. Their sample consists of 880 children between 2 and 12 years of age. Nelson (1962, in Rosenfeld et al., 1984) studied the modesty socialization of 44 upper-middle-class children below the age of 3. She finds that parents who encourage nudity are also more physically affectionate with their children. Parents who are restrictive about nudity report far less than more permissive parents that their children notice sex differences when other family members are naked. In a series of articles Rosenfeld and his colleagues published the results of a study of 576, 2- to-10-year-olds, most of them coming from upper-middle-class families. Children's touching of parental genitals and mothers' breasts is positively correlated with a child's bathing with parents (Rosenfeld, Bailey, Siegel, and Bailey, 1986). If children's curiosity is interpreted as sexual, parents stop bathing with their children or the bathing together of siblings is no longer allowed (Rosenfeld, Siegel, and Bailey, 1987).

By the reactions children provoke in other people when they try to explore their bodies (e.g., resistance, excitement), children acquire rules for physical interaction (e.g., touching, nudity), which may help them to protect their identity in later sexual interactions and to respect other people's privacy. There is growing literature on the development of shame and embarrassment as regulators of appropriate social behavior (e.g., Tangney and Fisher, 1995) which can be applied to explain the acquisition of sexual inhibition and modesty in children. Young children who do not follow the valid rules and standards of behavior for intimate situations in their social reference group are shamed by other children or adults. The older the children become the more the process of becoming ashamed is internalized and occurs without other people's intervention or even without their presence.

The representation of the sexual characteristics of children's bodies is fundamental to sex-related aspects of their identity. It may help them to stabilize their identity if they compare their bodies with those of other children and adults and identify themselves with persons of their own sex, not only by aspects of gender role, but also by the physical characteristics (the genitals) which they have in common with them. At the same time they can distinguish themselves from persons of the other sex. Kleeman expects that a child's "core gender identity" is already well established at the end of the third year of life; according to other authors a critical period for its formation is already reached by 18 months (see Kleeman, 1971). Parallel to the development of such a "core gender identity," a number of processes may take place which have been postulated by modern psychoanalytical theories as early as the second year of life: an oedipal constellation in the parent-child relationship, castration anxiety, genital envy, and feelings of inferiority in girls (Kleeman, 1975; Mertens, 1994; Roiphe and Galenson, 1981). Even if one does not agree with psychoanalytic theory in detail, it has helped to direct our awareness to possible differences in the sexual development of boys and girls and their interactions with mothers and fathers. In an empirical study on body discovery, especially of the sexual organs, one always has to have a look at the special dynamics in the relationships of persons of the same sex or of different sex in the family.

Children also expand their repertoire of sexual behavior when they are allowed to interact sexually with other children, and they learn something about the sensitivity and arousability of the sexual organs and may become very skillful in applying certain techniques at an early age. Langfeldt (1981) describes a subculture of Norwegian boys that practiced start-and-stop procedures while they masturbated each other and had good orgasmic control during sexual interactions with women when they were older.

The more children are allowed to explore the characteristics of their bodies and those of other people the easier it may be for them to understand any information on reproduction and birth that is given to them (see Volbert, this volume).

The goals of the study reported below are to describe the process of body discovery in early childhood longitudinally and to test the practicability of a certain method of data collection, the mediator approach. We are interested in a description of events in which children relate to their bodies or those of other people because the quality and the strength of representation of certain body parts in young children can probably be inferred from elements of these events, e.g., from the sensory channels that are used to gain information, the evaluations that are expressed by the children or other people, and the accessibility of body parts for the children. The results reported here will concentrate on the discovery of other people's genitals; only when it is especially relevant comparisons are made to children's interest in their own sexual parts.

METHODS

Sample

We studied 26 children in 25 families (1 pair of male twins; 11 girls, 15 boys) longitudinally during their second year of life (1986-1987) and again once in their sixth year of life (1991). The families were living in Bamberg, a middle-sized city in northern Bavaria, and in the surrounding area. Addresses of parents were taken from a bulletin published by the local marriage license bureau, containing notes on most children born in the local hospital, and from lists of birth preparation classes lead by midwives. The families were contacted first by letter and then by a telephone call, and an introductory visit. Twenty-three (27%) of the contacted families agreed to be in the study. Two more families volunteered after they had learned about the project from other people. The first detailed description of the study was given during the telephone call. It was announced as a project on body discovery in general and the genital aspect was not emphasized, as it might seem reading the article. The main reasons for not participating were the duration of the study (12 months) and the large amount of work involved. But in fact, the knowledge of body parts may have been a topic of higher valence for some parents, e.g., those working in the health sector who make up about one fifth of the parents in the sample.

The children of the sample had to fulfill certain criteria. They had to grow up in complete families and had to be cared for by their own parents regularly. Children were excluded if they showed signs of mental retardation or physical handicaps, if they were born before the 36th week or after the 42nd week of gestation, or if they had gone through a very complicated birth.

The families were from various social backgrounds, although mostly middle class. Twenty-three fathers were employed full time and two fathers were students. Fourteen mothers did not work, one was a student, and most of the others worked 20 hours or less; all mothers, except one, had completed a vocational training. Ten mothers and 12 fathers held a degree from high school, the rest had finished lower level types of schooling. The mothers were between 24 and 43 years old (Mean = 29 years, 5 months), the fathers were between 24 and 45 years old (Mean = 32 years, 2 months). At the end of their second year of life nine children had no siblings, the rest between 1 and 3 ($Mean_{children\ per\ family}$ = 1.9). The age of the siblings varied between 5 months and 20 years. At the second time of data collection, only three children remained without siblings.

Data Collection

The data collection took place in the family homes and started when the children were between 12 months, 3 days and 15 months of age (Mean = 12 months, 16 days). Data were obtained by observation of the children by a mediator–usually the mother, sometimes both parents and by interviews with the mother. Observation by a mediator seemed to be a good method to get constant observations, especially of intimate situations, e.g., the parents and the child sitting together in the bath tub, or when a behavior is expected to occur rarely (Selg, 1984). The parents were instructed to have a close look at all manifestations of what we called body discovery in their children directed to the children's own bodies and those of other people and to reactions of the children when other people did something to the children's bodies. The parents were supposed to report all situations which were in any respect new–a new type of behavior, place, context, person, etc. Written instructions were given to the parents: they were told which particular behavior they should be observing, how they should record their observations, and to record their observations as soon as possible, at the latest in the evening of the same day. The first attempts were discussed and corrected to increase the quality of the observations. The parents were supplied with small tape recorders to keep track of their observations, but some of them preferred to use paper and pencil. Every four to six weeks the researcher came to the family home and collected the papers or recordings, which were later transcribed and discussed with the mediators during the next visit of the researcher. Parents finished their observations after the second birthday of their children. When the children reached the age of 26 months, the interview was conducted in which questions were asked concerning children's opportunities to be naked and to see other people naked (in the bath or on the toilet); particular emphasis was placed on aspects of genital discovery. When the children were in their sixth year of life, we interviewed the mothers again.

Analysis of Data

The material collected by the parents contains not only specific reports, which means observations of events that took place at a certain day at a certain time, but also more generalized reports, which described how an event would normally progress over a certain period of time. The basic unit of analysis is an episode. [1] All episodes collected over the year and during the interview were coded according to a scheme which was based on Tharp and Wetzel's (1969) considerations of behavior analysis for the purpose of behavior modification. [2] Our coding scheme consisted of 16 columns each containing particular pieces of information on an episode:

1. number of episodes, classification as coming from a specific or generalized report
2. date of episode
3. age of child in months
4. day time
5. length of episode, frequency of certain aspects of episode
6. body parts to which behavior is directed
7. people to whom body parts belong
8. behavior of child directed to body parts, except emotion
9. what stimulates behavior directed to body parts
10. what sets an end to behavior directed to body parts or interrupts it
11. behavior of child before and during body-directed behavior
12. behavior of child after body-directed behavior
13. behavior of other people: body-directed or other
14. components of situation: persons present, place, context of behavior (e.g., diaper change), peculiarities of clothing, state of organism (e.g., being sick)
15. emotion of the child
16. comment: of mediator or scientist, antecedents and consequences of behavior in the long run, frequency of generalized episodes

A system of categories was also developed for the interviews from the second and sixth year of children's lives (Boehnstedt, 1992; Schuhrke, 1991). The interrater reliability was checked for extraction of relevant episodes from the observations and the interviews, for entering information into the correct columns of the behavior analytic scheme, and the correct categorization of other information from the interviews. [3]

Statistical analysis was performed with methods applicable to ordinal and nominal data: Kruskal-Wallis-H-test (Kruskal-Wallis, z), Mann-Whitney-U-test (z), Wilcoxon-test (T), Spearman rank correlation (r_s), Cureton-test (u) (Lienert, 1973, p. 332f), McNemar (χ^2), Fisher's exact probability (Fisher's exact prob., *p*), test in Darlington (1975, p. 472) (*p*). If not indicated otherwise all probabilities are reported for the 2-tailed test.

The reliability and validity of parents as mediators were checked at the end of the observation period (for details see Schuhrke, 1991). Although six of the mothers scored low on a reliability measure for the genital reports and four of them also on a validity measure for the genital reports, none of the families were exluded from the analysis. We decided that way because of the descriptive and exploratory nature of the study, the small sample size, and because part of the information was completed during the regular visits and by the interviews.

The reliability measure for the genital reports correlates positively with a measure for mothers' positive reaction to children's manipulations of their own genitals (r_s = .59, p ≤ .001). To exclude the less reliable mediators and their families could possibly have meant to get no observations at all from families with less liberal attitudes. The reliability and validity measures show no direct relationship to the educational level of the mediators (Kruskal-Wallis). However, the measure for mothers' positive reactions to children's manipulations of their own genitals correlates positively with the school education of the mediators (r_s = .38, p ≤ .03). Therefore it seems that there is at least an indirect influence of education on the reliability of the mediators conveyed by their formation of sexual attitudes. There are no differences in the reliability and validity of the reports on girls and boys, but there is a tendency to more reliable reports on the genital behavior of girls than of boys (z = − 1.72, p ≤ .09).

RESULTS

The terms interest, curiosity, or occupation are used to label the whole range of behavior directed toward the genitals of other people. Of 858 episodes describing genital-related experiences of children in the second year of life, 207 are relevant for the children's interest in other people. There are large differences in the number of episodes reported per child, but there were only two children (one girl, one boy) who seemed to be totally indifferent to other people during the whole year.

Behavioral Manifestations of Curiosity in the Second Year of Life

In the second year of life, there are a multitude of ways in which children encounter the genitals of other people. They can be organized into six types of behavioral manifestations:

1. *Looking and Manipulation*–contains visual attention and modes of attention by which it is not clear to what extent these are just glances or actual manipulation. However, a visual component is probably included in all cases (e.g., watch, explore, and show interest).
2. *Manipulation*–contains clear manipulation that has nothing to do with natural body care (e.g., submerge penis under water, pour water over it, hold it, move it from one side to the other; touch, pet, grab, smack, feel, pull genital organs; press and push the skin of the female organ, tickle it).
3. *Cover and Uncover*–contains attempts by the children to expose genitals (e.g., open dress and reach into dress) or else to cover them.
4. *Body Care*–comprised of body care activities (e.g., to apply skin care and to wipe). However, it is uncertain as to whether or not the children performed these activities with the actual intention of body care. The actions performed could just as well have been forms of information seeking or stimulation, as in the manipulation of type 2.
5. *Acquaintance*–includes behavior which illustrates that the children are familiar with the sex organs, that they can refer to them verbally or non-verbally, and that they can make verbal or non-verbal comparisons of their sex organs with those of people of the same or opposite sex (e.g., to show, to name, and to compare).
6. *Comments*–consists of various verbal comments regarding function, manipulations of the child, and sensations other people experience in their genital area (e.g., capability to urinate).

The following examples illustrate the interest of a 17-month-old girl (K) in her brother (B) and an 18-month-old boy (G) in his sister (M). They show a high degree of understanding at an early age. Both children compare their genital region with the appropriate region in siblings of the other sex and both are probably aware of the different make-up of their bodies. While K can already express herself verbally very well, G's speech develops slowly and until the end of the second year much of his understanding is shown by nonverbal behavior (gestures, facial expression, sounds).

Observation 1: It occurred to me today that when K bathes (note: when both are in the bathtub together) she always wants to touch B's penis and sometimes B also touches her; another thing which happened is that she said, "B peepee; B peepee hide" and then she held her hand in front of B's penis and said, "B girl." I figure that she thinks once the peepee is gone then B is also a girl.

Observation 2: After her evening bath, I dry M. G comes and observes M's naked body. Then he looks at me and points to M's navel. I nod to G and say, "That's the belly button." Then G squats and looks at M's behind. He points to M's vagina and gently touches her. He then looks down at himself and points to his genitalia. Then he touches her navel again.

The following kinds of behavior (belonging to type 1, 2, and 5, see above) are the most common ones as they were shown by more than half of the girls or boys sampled. More than half of the boys watch the female genitals, watch the male genitals, and/or touch the male genitals. Naming of the male genitals by boys occurs in slightly less than half. More than half of the girls name the female genitals, name the male genitals, watch the male genitals, and/or are interested in them. Touching of the male genitals by girls also occurs in slightly less than half.

Three of the girls also apply certain kinds of behavior to their dolls, i.e., they name the genital area with their word for the female sex organ, clean it, or comment on what they are doing.

In males, the attention of the children is almost exclusively directed toward the penis and not to the testes or the pubic hair. In females, children are mostly curious about the pubic hair and the genital area as a whole. One girl tried to manipulate the clitoris of another girl. She had been very active in exploring her own genital area before and had already discovered her clitoris. Overall, interest is similarly distributed when children turn to their own bodies, with more activity directed toward the clitoris and, of course, with the exception of the pubic hair.

When children are occupied with their own bodies, they quite often use objects for manipulation (e.g., stuffed animals, tooth brushes, and building blocks) or body care. This is very rare, however, when they are occupied with other people's bodies, the only objects used for manipulation being water, toilet paper, and healing ointment.

One very common behavior is the naming of the genitals. The first words children use for their own genitals are quite often not specific for the genitals, but are derived from the child's word for urine or adjacent body parts (belly or buttocks). Sometimes the same word is used for the genitals of both sexes. The spontaneous use of specific names for the genitals of other people was also investigated. Specific words for the female genitals are only found in four girls, for the male genitals in seven boys and four girls. In most cases these words are applied for the first time during the second half of the second year, but in some cases they are already mentioned within the 16th month. Specific names for the children's genitals are used earlier than specific words for other people's genitals ($n = 15$; $p \leq .01$). [4] Nine children have neither a specific word for their own genitals nor for those of other people. Two cases were excluded from the analysis because of problems in dating the first episodes.

Signs of emotional expression or arousal may be very important to determine how children evaluate their experiences with other people's genitals. No signs of sexual arousal are found, but rather positive (e.g., joy, laughter, enthusiasm, or fascination), or neutral (e.g., surprise or waiting with bated breath), or negative emotions (crying, cautious, afraid to do something, embarrassed, or uncomfortable) in some children. Parents do not see any signs of genital envy in their children's emotional reactions.

During experiences with the female genitals three girls and three boys react with positive or neutral emotions, and during experiences with the male genitals seven girls and eight boys react this way. Negative emotions are found in three children in situations in which the female genitals are explored and in two children when the male genitals are explored. The following example illustrates the interest of a little girl (C) of 23 months in her father (F).

Observation: C had become aware for the first time of F's penis. It was in the bathroom and F had changed C and placed her on the floor and wanted to get dressed himself. It was in the morning and he wasn't wearing any pyjamas. C pointed to his penis and said, "Daddy is?" F said that it was his penis. F said, she wanted to know what it did and he told her that "peepee" came out of it. C asked, "Make?" Then she wanted to touch it and was a little bit surprised that it felt so funny. F tolerated it. She was very careful, more careful than she was when she examined other things. She also touched the testicles. For a few days afterwards, she always wanted to see his penis, which F allowed. A similar scene occurred every day when F got dressed. Her fascination lasted about 8 to 10 days before her interest passed again.

Curiosity and Type of Person in the Second Year of Life

According to our findings, occupation with one's own body seems to be an important forerunner of the occupation with other people's bodies. The children discover their own genitals earlier than those of other people ($n = 25$, $p \leq .001$). [4] In one case the first events cannot exactly be dated.

In the second year of life, children turn to both parents, siblings, and in some cases to children and adults who do not belong to the family. Almost always the interest in parents' bodies precedes the interest in those of siblings and other children ($n = 23$, $p \leq .01$). [4] One child was excluded from the comparison because of problems in dating the first episodes. Twenty-four children are interested in their fathers and 20 children in their mothers. The median age for the first interest in fathers and mothers is 18 months ($range_F = 13$ to > 26 months, $range_M = 14$ to > 26 months), interest in girls 21 months (7 children; range = 17 to > 26 months), and interest in boys 20 months 15 days (12 children; range = 13 to > 26 months). [5]

Two variables can be expected to exert an important influence on the sexual curiosity of children: their own gender and the gender of the person their curiosity is directed toward. Children's curiosity, in terms of motivation, could be aroused by the type of genitals being unfamiliar to them, different from their own genitals. In this case, the other-sex parent should be preferred. Or the curiosity could be aroused by the visually more conspicuous organ, which means that all children should prefer the male genitals. Another motivation of children's curiosity might be provided for by early processes of identification. If that is the case, children should prefer the genitals of their own sex. To test these hypotheses, we use the number of different types of behavior the children show toward their fathers and mothers as an indicator of children's strength of interest. The following results were obtained: boys' same-sex interest is as strong as girls' same-sex-interest ($z = 1.08$, n.s.); boys' other-sex interest is less strong than girls' other-sex-interest ($z = -2.41$, $p \leq .05$); boys' same-sex interest is stronger than boys' other-sex interest ($T = 7, p \leq .05$), and girls' same-sex interest is as strong as girls' other-sex interest ($T = 11$, n.s.). In terms of number of children, however, there is no difference between children's interest in mothers and fathers (χ^2 (1, $N = 26$) = 0, 1-tailed, n.s.). If we take other people into account besides the parents (e.g., siblings and other children), there is only a statistical trend, especially for girls, to show more intense curiosity toward the male genitals (girls: $u = 1.87$, $p \leq .06$; boys: $u = 1.44$, $p \leq .13$, n.s.). More girls than boys are interested in children of the other sex (Fisher's exact prob., $p \leq .05$). Male genitals are visually more conspicuous and therefore seem to stimulate children more to explore them. In addition, the girls in this sample seem to be more active than the boys.

Changes in Curiosity from the Second to the Sixth Year of Life

Because parents did not observe their children in the sixth year of life, the data on children's curiosity behavior are not as detailed. Only three behavioral categories can be differentiated, which combine the former six types: Looking and manipulation (type 1), manipulation (types 2, 3, and 4), and verbalization (types 5 and 6).

In the following analysis, the changes in overall interest and manipulation from the second to the sixth year of life will be examined. Until the sixth year of life, the parents of all children noticed curiosity about the genitals of other people in their children. Only two children never tried to manipulate the genitals of other people.

Over the years, a decrease in the children's interest in their parents can be expected; but no significant changes in the number of boys or girls who were interested in their mothers' genitals or in the number of girls who are interested in their fathers' genitals were found. Only the interest of boys in their fathers diminished significantly (χ^2 (1, $N = 26$) = 3.6, 1-tailed, $p \leq .05$).

The curiosity in siblings is difficult to evaluate. Number and gender constellation of the siblings changed in many families from the first time of data collection to the second. Furthermore, children's contact to other children outside the family might have compensated for their lack of opportunities to satisfy their curiosity in the family. As was expected, more children were interested in children outside the family at the second time of data collection (χ^2 (1, $N = 26$) = 8.1, 1-tailed, $p \leq .01$).

Overall there are still as many children interested in parents as in children outside the family and siblings taken together (12 in girls, 18 in boys, 15 in mothers, and 16 in fathers).

Opportunities to Explore the Genitals in the Second and Sixth Year of Life

In which types of situations do children turn their attention to other people's genitals? In the second year of life, their curiosity is mostly aroused when other people are naked. In 80% of the observed episodes other people are undressed, at least in the genital area. The most important situations are going to the toilet, followed by somebody washing himself or taking a shower or bath, and walking around the house nude. Other types of situations are reported more rarely. Typically the first curiosity in others, especially in males, is awakened when the children watched them urinating.

Only in 25% of the episodes do parents explicitly mention what ended children's exploration behavior in that specific episode. In about half of the reported activities other people initiate the discontinuation: by continuing their activities (e.g. finish urinating or dressing), by verbal or physical interventions, by leaving the situation, or by distracting the child.

In the second year of life, all girls and boys join their parents, at least on occasion, when they go to the toilet. As expected, these numbers are significantly reduced four years later, especially for fathers (χ^2M $(1, N = 26) = 3.6, \chi^2$F $(1, N = 26) = 2.7$, 1-tailed, $p \leq .05$). As the children's mothers report, 7 girls and 13 boys join their mothers and six girls and six boys join their fathers. In the second year of life, 12 children have the opportunity to be in the room while adults, who do not belong to the nuclear family, use the toilet; no similar experience, however, is reported for older children.

The results show a different development for the second important situation in which children have the opportunity to learn something about other people's private parts. In the second year of life, nine girls and nine boys sometimes take a shower or bath together with their mothers, and the same numbers are true for fathers. Four years later the numbers do not show much change. In families where a parent takes a bath or shower with the child in the second year of life, the same holds true in the sixth year of life; in families where this does not happen in the younger years parents do not change their habit in the later years (χ^2M $(1, N = 26) = 0, \chi^2$F $(1, N = 26) = 0.11$, 1-tailed, n.s.).

These results do not say anything about changes in frequency. If there are siblings, children take their baths exclusively or most of the time with them; this is the case for both the first and the second data collection. In the sixth year of life, 19 children share the tub with siblings. At both times of data collection, all children are allowed to come into the bathroom when other members of the family are taking a bath or a shower.

DISCUSSION

The results show that curiosity about other people's genitals is a quite general phenomena in children who have at least some opportunity for exploration. Nudity of other people is an important prerequisite for an early interest to occur, and the most common situations in which genital nudity occurs in the family are the most important situations for a child's sexual curiosity: going to the toilet or cleaning the body. But sheer nudity is probably not the main eliciting factor for children's interest. As mentioned in the introduction, the function of an organ is important for its meaning, and the earliest function children can connect with the genitals is the elimination of urine, especially at a time when they become more aware and gain more control of their elimination of wastes (see also Roiphe and Galenson, 1981). The more common and earlier interest in the parental genitals compared to other children's genitals is probably aroused by the size and strange appearance of the adult genitals which makes them very different from the children's ones.

Our results support the expectation that the children's occupation with their own genitals is a developmental forerunner of the occupation with the genitals of other people. In some cases, exactly the same behavior is applied to the child's body and to the bodies of other people. But it is not certain which kind of a link exists: is a child's interest in his own body a necessary condition for his interest in other people's bodies to occur or does it only have a facilitating influence?

The parents are important objects of sexual curiosity even in the preschool years. It is questionable, whether the information that is provided by the appearance of their nude bodies, by their allowing for and setting limits to physical manipulation, can be replaced by experiences with other children. Insofar as parents can be behavioral models concerning telling the truth, keeping promises and other moral values, they can be models for both careful handling of other people's bodies and for setting and accepting boundaries to physical exchange. The parents' physical appearance points to the child's future, to adulthood, something that the experience with peers cannot offer. Therefore the exploration of the parental body may give children the opportunity to connect more theoretical knowledge they gain about reproduction later on at least to some realistic experience with other people's bodies. But probably many modern parents find themselves confronted with different demands: to give their children a basically good feeling about matters of sexuality, to protect their own physical privacy, and to avoid any behavior that might be interpreted as incestuous or sexually overstimulating for their children.

The increase in the number of children from the second to the sixth year who are interested in the genitals of other children, parallels the growing influence of the peer group in general. Interactions on a more equal level of knowledge and power may take place, possibly based on standards which have already been established in the parent-child interaction.

The more intense curiosity about the male genitals in the second year, which is indicated by a greater diversity of behavior and a better knowledge of names, can be attributed to the greater visual conspicuousness of the male genitals. On average, the boys seem less interested and less knowledgeable about the female genitals, while the girls seem to be more equally interested in both sexes. Even by the time when boys are six years old, they have not caught up with girls' other-sex interest. One can expect girls to have a better body representation of the other sex than boys.

The most obvious decrease in sexual curiosity from early childhood to the preschool years takes place between fathers and sons. Most of the observations on fathers are reported by mothers. Therefore it is more difficult to learn something about the underlying dynamics: how much has to be attributed to a reduction in children's motivation and how much to an increase in fathers' reserve about their sons' curiosity. From a psychoanalytic point of view the decrease of a boy's sexual interest in his father may signify the mastery of the oedipal situation. Rosenfeld et al. (1984) cite other authors who state, in contrast to their own findings, an essentially homosexual sex anxiety in men which may explain the growing distance of sons and fathers found in our study. However, the boys become more and more involved with boys from their peer group which may partially substitute for the sexual interest in their fathers. Everyday observations give the impression of a strong interest in each other's genitals among boys of preschool age and above, including elements of competition and rivalry. [6]

The observations during the second year show a diversity of behavior, but still this diversity is less compared to the many different kinds of behavior children try out on their own bodies (Schuhrke, 1991). Maybe there are already very particular feelings about nude bodies as vulnerable or strange which ensure a certain amount of respect or reservation without children having developed mature rules of modesty. Also "social referencing" may take place, a process which is already well-established in one-year-old children. When they approach new or forbidden objects, they look to their care-takers for an emotional reaction and regulate their behavior according to the perceived emotional signs (see Emde and Oppenheim, 1995). Nevertheless, children make attempts to touch the genitals of other people both in the second and in the sixth year of life, and Rosenfeld et al. (1986) report that touching of parental genitals by children is not uncommon, even in older age groups.

The results from typical situations in which children explore other people's bodies show that there is probably a stronger taboo or more body shame concerning the anal zone than there is concerning the genital zone. While the families are quite open about nudity at both times of data collection, the presence of children is reduced in the sixth year when other people go to the toilet. Results from a newer study on body shame show that parents find it more disturbing when children are in the room during defecation than during urination (Schuhrke, 1996). In the study of Rosenfeld et al. (1984) more families had particular rules regarding toilet practices than regarding nudity.

Methodological Problems

The tendency of mothers of girls to be more reliable observers and to hold more favorable attitudes towards their daughters' genital self-discovery may point to a certain problem. Maybe the girl-families of the sample are a more liberal subgroup of all girl-families than the boy-families are of all boy-families. In that case, the curiosity of girls would be overestimated in comparison to the boys. In fact, it was somewhat more difficult to recruit girl-families for the study than boy-families.

It was a twofold advantage that parents observed the discovery of the whole body: it was probably a more acceptable topic to some of the families, and it made it possible to compare the discovery of different body parts (Schuhrke, 1991). The disadvantage was that the task of observation became more difficult. To a certain extent decreases in quality of observation were determined by unforeseeable life events: disease, death, and house construction. The regular visits of the researcher were important for the motivation, although briefer intervals might have been even better. Overall, the observation by parents combined with interview strategies seems to be a valuable approach to lay a descriptive foundation in an otherwise not well-studied field.

NOTES

1. An episode contains all behavior directed to a body which appeared at the same time or within brief intervals of time at the same place or during a continuous movement from one place to another. There must be at least three types of information as core of an episode: (1) a behavior of the child directed to his own body or the body of another person, or a behavior of another person directed to the child's body, (2) a person to whom the behavior is directed and a person who shows a behavior, (3) body parts by which the behavior is managed and body parts to which the behavior is directed. A generalized report was treated as if it described a specific event. The term 'behavior' is used for all kinds of activities, including deeds, perceptions, cognitions, and emotions.

2. This particular way of data analysis was already prepared by the instructions parents had been given for their observations.

3. We calculated the interrater reliability according to Holsti: The percentage of shared decisions of two raters. From the observations we took the material of 31 consecutive days from each family (449 episodes). The reliability for extraction of episodes was 85%. For the behavior analytic scheme the reliability was for all columns except for one between 82 and 90%. For stimulants of body-directed behavior it was only 74%. We checked the reliability for 4 (2nd year)/5 (6th year) interviews. It varied between 70/71 and 92/100% for the different questions, almost always it was between 80/80 and 90/100%.

4. If a child names his own genitals for the first time at a certain age and names the genitals of other people later, this means that the naming of his own genitals occurred earlier. If a child names his own genitals and does not name the genitals of other people, this also means that the naming of his own genitals occurred earlier. The statistical comparison was performed in the same way when the relevant behavior was not naming but interest in other people's genitals in general or when the interest in different kinds of people was compared.

5. For the calculation of the median, we only used the data of the children who developed an interest during the period of observation. In the information on the

range, all children are included: a theoretical value of '> 26 months' means 'no interest during the period of observation until the final interview.'

6. The basis are everyday observations of the author and reports of members of the staff of a day-care center (Neubauer, 1993).

REFERENCES

Boehnstedt, T. (1992). *Koerperkontakt und Sexualitaet Fuenf-bis Sechsjaehriger aus der Sicht ihrer Muetter: Bezugspersonen, Interesse, Wissen, Erfahrungen, Grenzen* [Physical contact and sexuality of five-to-six-year-olds from the view of their mothers: Care-Takers, interest, knowledge, experiences, limitations]. Unveroeff. Diplomarbeit, Universitaet Bamberg.

Darlington, R.B. (1975). *Radicals and squares.* Statistical methods for the behavioral sciences. Ithaca, NY: Logan Hill.

Emde, R.N., and Oppenheim, D. (1995). Shame, guilt, and the oedipal drama: Developmental considerations concerning morality and the referencing of critical others. In J.P. Tangney and K.W. Fischer (Eds.), *Self-conscious emotions: The psychology of shame, guilt, embarrassment, and pride* (pp. 413-436). New York: The Guilford Press.

Fisher, S. (1970). *Body experience in phantasy and behavior.* New York: Appleton.

Fisher, S. (1989). *Sexual images of the self. The psychology of erotic sensations and illusions.* Hillsdale, NJ: Erlbaum.

Fisher, S., and Cleveland, S.E. (1968). *Body image and personality.* Princeton, NJ: van Nostrand.

Friedrich, W.N., Grambsch, P., Broughton, D., Kuiper, J., and Beilke, R.L. (1991). Normative sexual behavior in children. *Pediatrics, 88*, 456-464.

Head, H., and Holmes, G. (1911/12). Sensory disturbances from cerebral brain lesions. *Brain, 34*, 102-245.

Kleeman, J.M. (1971). The establishment of core gender identity in normal girls II: How meanings are conveyed between parent and child in the first 3 years. *Archives of Sexual Behavior, 2*, 117-129.

Kleeman, J.M. (1975). Genital self-stimulation in infant and toddler girls. In I. Marcus, and J. Francis (Eds.), *Masturbation from infancy to senescence* (pp. 77-106). New York: International Universities Press.

Kolb, L.C. (1975). Disturbances of the body image. In S. Arieti (Ed.), *American Handbook of Psychiatry* (Vol. IV, 2nd Ed., pp. 810-837). New York: Basic Books.

Langfeldt, T. (1981). Childhood masturbation. Individual and social organisation. In L.L. Constantine, and F.M. Martinson (Eds.), *Children and sex: New findings, new perspectives* (pp. 37-44). Boston, MA: Little, Brown, and Company.

Lemche, E. (1993). *Das Koerperbild in der psychoanalytischen Entwicklungspsychologie* [The body image in psychoanalytic developmental psychology]. Eschborn: Verlag Dietmar Klotz.

Lewis, R.J., and Janda, L.H. (1988). The relationship between sexual adjustment and childhood experiences regarding exposure to nudity, sleeping in the parental bed, and parental attitudes toward sexuality. *Archives of Sexual Behavior, 17*, 349-362.

Lienert, G.A. (1973). *Verteilungsfreie Methoden in der Biostatistik* [Distribution-Free methods in biostatistics] (Bd.1). Meisenheim am Glan: Hain.

Mertens, W. (1994). *Entwicklung der Psychosexualitaet und der Geschlechtsidentitaet* [Development of psychosexuality and sexual identity] (Bd. 1, 2. Aufl.). Stuttgart: Kohlhammer.

Neubauer, G. (1993). "Sex" im Kinderhaus: Auch kleine Jungen tun's! ["Sex" in a day-care center: Young boys also do it!] In R. Winter (Hrsg.). *Stehversuche. Sexuelle Jungensozialisation und maennliche Lebensbewaeltigung durch Sexualitaet.* Tuebingen: Neuling.

Poeck, K., and Orgass, B. (1964). Ueber die Entwicklung des Koerperschemas: Untersuchungen an gesunden, blinden und amputierten Kindern [On the development of the body scheme: Studies with healthy, blind, and amputated children]. *Fortschritte der Neurologie und Psychiatrie, 32*, 538-555.

Provence, S., and Lipton, R.D. (1962). *Infants in institutions.* New York: International Universities Press.

Roiphe, H., and Galenson, E. (1981). *Infantile origins of sexual identity.* New York: International Universities Press.

Rosenfeld, A., Bailey, R., Siegel, B., and Bailey, G. (1986). Determining incestuous contact between parent and child: Frequency of children touching parents' genitals in a nonclinical population. *Journal of the American Academy of Child Psychiatry, 25*, 481-484.

Rosenfeld, A.A., Siegel, B., and Bailey, R. (1987). Familial bathing patterns: Implications for cases of alleged molestation and for pediatric practice. *Pediatrics, 79*, 224-229.

Rosenfeld, A., Siegel-Gorelick, B., Haavik, D., Duryea, M., Wenegrat, A., Martin, J., and Bailey, R. (1984). Parental perceptions of children's modesty: A cross-sectional survey of ages two to ten years. *Psychiatry, 47*, 351-365.

Schilder, P. (1950). *The image and appearance of the human body.* New York: International Universities Press.

Schuhrke, B. (1991). *Koerperentdecken und psychosexuelle Entwicklung: Theoretische Ueberlegungen und eine Laengsschnittuntersuchung an Kindern im zweiten Lebensjahr* [Body discovery and psychosexual development: Theoretical considerations and a longitudinal study of children in their second year of life]. Regensburg: Roderer.

Schuhrke, B. (1996). *Shame of urination and defecation in 2-to 9-year-old children.* Poster presented at the 22nd Annual Meeting of the International Academy of Sex Research, Rotterdam, June 26-30.

Shontz, F.C. (1974). Body image and its disorders. *International Journal of Psychiatry in Medicine, 5*, 461-472.

Selg, H. (1984). Mediatorenmodelle in der Verhaltensbeobachtung–Moeglichkeiten in schwer zugaenglichen Feldern [Mediator approaches to the observation of behavior–chances for inaccessible fields of study]. *Zeitschrift fuer Personenzentrierte Psychologie und Psychotherapie, 3*, 67-71.

Spitz, R.A., and Wolf, K.M. (1949). Autoerotism. *The Psychoanalytic Study of the Child, 3/4*, 85-120.

Tangney, J.P., and Fischer, K.W. (Eds.). (1995). *Self-conscious emotions: The psychology of shame, guilt, embarrassment, and pride.* New York: The Guilford Press.

Tharp, R.G., and Wetzel, R.J. (1969). *Behavior modification in the natural environment.* New York, Academic Press.

Studying Children's Sexuality
from the Child's Perspective

Jany Rademakers, PhD
Marjoke Laan, PhD candidate
Cees J. Straver, PhD, LLM

ABSTRACT. In an exploratory study on body awareness and experiences with physical intimacy from children's own perspective, 16 boys and 15 girls (age 8/9) were interviewed. Almost all children displayed a positive attitude towards intimate physical contact, especially cuddling. Half of the children didn't report experiences regarding sexuality or physical intimacy with peers, while one third displayed an active interest in these, had their own experiences and were able to reflect on those. A few children had a negative or ambivalent attitude towards physical intimacy. Data were also collected from one of the parents of each child. Parents presented a more positive and permissive view of the situation at home regarding physical intimacy than children did. *[Article copies available for a fee from The Haworth Document Delivery Service: 1-800-342-9678. E-mail address: <getinfo@haworthpressinc.com> Website: <http://www.HaworthPress.com>]*

KEYWORDS. Child sexuality, sexual development, parent-child interaction, methodology

---

Jany Rademakers is Coordinator of the Research Program "Sexuality and the Life Cycle," the Netherlands Institute of Social Sexological Research (NISSO), Utrecht, the Netherlands. Marjoke Laan was temporarily affiliated with NISSO as Research Associate. Cees J. Straver is Senior Advisor at NISSO.

Address correspondence to Jany Rademakers, NISSO, Oudenoord 182, 3513 EV Utrecht, the Netherlands.

[Haworth co-indexing entry note]: "Studying Children's Sexuality from the Child's Perspective." Rademakers, Jany, Marjoke Laan, and Cees J. Straver. Co-published simultaneously in *Journal of Psychology & Human Sexuality* (The Haworth Press, Inc.) Vol. 12, No. 1/2, 2000, pp. 49-60; and: *Childhood Sexuality: Normal Sexual Behavior and Development* (ed: Theo G. M. Sandfort, and Jany Rademakers) The Haworth Press, Inc., 2000, pp. 49-60. Single or multiple copies of this article are available for a fee from The Haworth Document Delivery Service [1-800-342-9678, 9:00 a.m. - 5:00 p.m. (EST). E-mail address: getinfo@haworthpressinc.com].

INTRODUCTION

Sexuality and the normal sexual development of children under the age of 12 have long been neglected topics in scientific studies. As a result of this, theory, empirical data and methodological knowledge in this area remain scarce (Laan 1994, Van der Zanden 1992, Sandfort 1989, Constantine and Martinson 1981). This lack in knowledge about normal sexual behavior of children is felt even more strongly since child sexual abuse has become an important theme in debate, counselling and research in the past decade. Criteria about what was to be considered *normal* and *abnormal* had to be established, since abnormal sexual interest and behavior is regarded as an indication that a child had been abused.

Defining and operationalizing sexuality is one of the problems which has to be addressed when studying children's sexuality (Frayser 1995). The concepts of sexuality often used in studies with adults are generally of little use in research with children. The limited definition of human sexuality in terms of the sexual response cycle (desire, excitement, orgasm) doesn't do justice to aspects of sexuality which are more relevant to children. Generally in sexological literature, three aspects of sexuality are distinguished: (1) biological sexual differentiation and psychological gender; (2) body awareness and physical sexual responsiveness; and (3) intimacy and capacity to form close relationships (Bancroft 1989). Most of the research with children has focused on sexual differentation and the development of gender identity and roles. Body awareness, sexual responsiveness and aspects of intimacy have seldom been studied in this age group.

Methodological problems also hamper this line of research. Observation and retrospective studies are the most frequently used methods to study childhood sexuality, but they have some obvious limitations. Addressing children directly is very difficult as well. Young children don't have the verbal capacities to express themselves on these issues, and until age 7 or 8 boys and girls are not able to reflect on topics from a more abstract level. New instruments have to be developed, and questions about the validity and reliability of these instruments have to be faced.

Within this context, a small size exploratory study on body awareness and experiences with physical intimacy from children's own perspective was conducted. The purpose of the study was to gain more insight in the way children experience their own body, their experiences with and appreciation of (non-intimate and intimate) physical contact with peers and parents and their experiences with one specific aspect of intimacy, e.g., being in love. A second purpose of the study was to determine whether parents know about the way their child experiences and appreciates physical contact and intimacy. Furthermore, the study was conducted with the aim to generate more knowledge about methodological aspects of sex research with children. More specific, the feasibility and usefulness of the research method used in this study was evaluated.

STUDY DESIGN AND METHODS

Because of the exploratory nature of the study and the focus on children's own perspective, a qualitative study design was chosen. A sample of 15 girls and 16 boys were interviewed about body awareness and their experiences with physical intimacy. Because the children had to master verbal and reflexive skills to a certain degree and the developmental differences within the sample shouldn't be too large, the decision was made to select only children of 8 and 9 years old. The children were contacted in the context of a routine school medical examination. In a semi-structured interview situation a female interviewer talked with the children about romping (as a non-intimate form of physical contact), cuddling and being in love. Furthermore the children were invited to mark on drawings of a same sex naked child's body which parts they considered *pleasant* and which parts they found *exciting*. The children were also asked to tell stories on the basis of four drawings which portrayed scenes like playing doctor or having a bath with an adult. They were asked about their own experiences in this respect. All parts of the research instrument were pretested in this age group. The children were alone in the room with the interviewer. The interview was taped. Children were assured that the information they gave would be kept confidential. On average, the interviews took about 20 minutes. The data were analysed qualitatively. After a preliminary coding of the material, categories were made per theme on the basis of the content of the answers. The number of children whose answers fitted in these categories were counted.

Data were also collected from the parents of the children. During the time the child was interviewed, in another room, one of the parents of each child (26 mothers, 4 fathers, 1 refusal) filled out a structured questionnaire which contained questions about similar topics that were discussed with the children. Additionally, some questions were asked about their attitudes and behavior with respect to the sexual development of their children. The data of the parents as a group were compared to the data of the children.

An elaborate description of the study design and the research instrument is presented in Laan (1994).

RESULTS

Romping

For a neutral, non-offensive start of the interview the children were asked about their experiences with and appreciation of romping. Half of the children (8 girls, 7 boys) described romping as pretend-fighting, something that involves the whole of the body. They stressed the wild movements and elaborated on pillow fights and games where they threw each other on the ground. This kind of romping was seen as positive.

> Romping is something I often do with my father, because I think it's fun and my father thinks it's fun and then we do it on my father's bed. (girl)

One-third (5 girls, 4 boys) saw romping as real fighting. They mentioned specific physical aggressive behavior, such as kicking, hitting and biting. Usually, the fighting was preceded by a quarrel and it ended with bruises and pain. Nobody liked this kind of romping.

> Romping, that is kicking and hitting and stuff. Romping hurts. (girl)

The other children (1 girl, 4 boys) saw romping variously as pretend and real. The pretend-fighting was generally done with parents, brothers and sisters, grandparents and peers. Real fighting took place with peers or elder children from school or the neighborhood.

Cuddling

The children were very unanimous in their description of cuddling. Apart from one boy, who didn't know what it was and after an explanation of the interviewer stated that he had never done such a thing, all other children (15 girls, 15 boys) mentioned hugging, kissing and sitting on someone's lap. Almost all of them regarded cuddling as something positive, either because of the bodily sensations cuddling produces, or because of the feeling of safety it gives them. They express their feelings regarding cuddling as safe, nice, soft, cheerful, fun, kind and comforting.

> If you like each other then you start cuddling, that is without words, in fact you use your whole body and that feels good everywhere. (girl)

> It feels soft at your belly and face, but it's not fun when she holds you too tight. (girl)

Only one boy felt negative about cuddling. He told about several occasions in which someone forced him to cuddle when he didn't want to. As with romping, the whole body is being used when cuddling. But here the children stressed the softness and tranquility of the movements. Half of the children (n = 15) cuddled with both humans and cuddly toys, dolls or stuffed animals. One third (n = 9) only cuddled with people. Generally, these people are close relatives such as brothers and sisters and grandparents. One child mentioned peers. Five children stated they only cuddled with toys, dolls or stuffed animals, and never with people.

Being in Love

When the theme 'being in love' was introduced in the interview, the atmosphere often changed. The questions about this theme elicited some tension, which was evident in non-verbal signs like giggling, sighing and voice changes. The way children described being in love differed from the way they had described romping and cuddling. While these two themes were defined by the children in terms of active behavior, being in love is a state which elicits bodily sensations such as blushing and tickling feelings in your belly.

Almost half of the children (8 girls, 5 boys) described being in love in terms of feelings.

> That you're crazy about a girl, and that when you see her it
> happens at once . . . you feel it near your heart, and you get red
> all over, and I immediately look the other way. (boy)

The other half (7 girls, 10 boys) gave a more factual description.

> That is two people who are friends for a long time and then they
> go steady and then they fall in love and then they get married.
> (girl)

One boy was not able to give a definition of 'being in love.'

More than half of these 8- and 9-year old children (n = 18) say they
are in love at the moment or have been in love before. Only one girl
reported being in love with another girl, the others were in love with
someone from the opposite sex. Most of the children who had experience with being in love also had fantasies about the person they're in
love with. Some of these fantasies had physical aspects:

> During the day, when she's away, I think, I wish she was here.
> And at night, in bed I wish she had been in bed with me, just to
> hold her. (boy)

Some had somewhat more 'innocent' wishes:

> Yes, I thought about it every night, about whom you're in love
> with, to play with her, because we're both too shy to play with
> each other. (boy)

The vast majority of the children (n = 23)–even some children who
didn't have experience with it themselves–reported being in love to be
a positive feeling. They mentioned it's good, fun and nice, it's a
tickling sensation and it makes you feel proud. Three children thought
it's negative, they didn't have any experience with it and they were not
interested in it either. The other children had no opinion in this respect.

Though being in love is generally regarded as a positive experience,
most of the children (n = 22) said they wouldn't tell anyone when
they're in love. The reason they unanimously gave for this taciturnity
is the fact other children and adults would tease them.

Pleasant and Exciting Body Parts

On a drawing of a same sex naked child's body the children were
asked to mark which parts they considered to be *pleasant*. No further

definition of 'pleasant' was offered. All children except one were able to indicate such parts. On a second drawing they were invited to mark *exciting* body parts, also without further definition. This was a more difficult task for the children. Nevertheless, most children (n = 25) also indicated such parts. The distinction between these two categories was made because whereas *pleasant* is considered to be a more general positive label, *exciting* more explicitly has an erotic or sexual connotation.

There was no difference in the order of children's indication of pleasant and exciting body parts (Table 1). In both categories, head and shoulders were the definite number one whereas arms and legs, belly and back, and chest were in the middle position. Genitals, bottom and anus were least indicated. There was also no difference in the indications of boys and girls.

Three Groups of Children

All in all, on the basis of their answers, the children can be grouped into three categories. Half of the total group (16 children) presented a positive attitude towards intimate physical contact, especially cuddling, but was relatively uninterested in the idea of being in love. Most of them also didn't have experience in this respect, and the tension which accompanied this theme in other interviews was absent with them.

The second category of 11 children had a positive attitude towards physical intimacy and displayed an active personal interest in the theme of being in love. All these children had been in love once or more, and they were able to talk about their behavior, feelings and motives. In terms of sexual development, this group seemed to be a step further than the first group.

The third and smallest group of 4 children gave indications of

TABLE 1. Pleasant and exciting body parts as indicated by the children (in n)

	pleasant	exciting
head and shoulders	24	18
arms and legs	15	17
belly and back	15	14
chest	11	13
genitals, bottom and anus	7	10

wanting to avoid certain topics or whose answers were very different from the rest of the group–for example, the boy who didn't know what cuddling was or the boy who felt negative about cuddling because it was forced upon him.

Discrepancies Between the Answers of Parents and Children

As a second part of the analysis, the information from the children was compared to the answers their parents gave. There were some interesting discrepancies between the data from these two sources.

The parents systematically report more occurrences of (non-intimate and intimate) physical contact between parent and child than the children do. Many more parents than children reported to engage in romping with their child. While almost all parents stated that they and/or their partner romped with the children, only half of the children reported romping with (one of) their parents. The same tendency was observed for cuddling: while all parents reported cuddling with their child, six children said this never happened.

Furthermore, the parents were asked whether they or their partner showered or bathed together with the child. With the help of a picture of a bathing scene, the children were asked the same question. Whereas three-quarters of the children said this never happened, less than two thirds of the parents answered they themselves did bathe together with the child, and almost half claimed their partner did.

Three parents (of n = 30) admitted they sometimes feel uneasy about being physically intimate with their child. The same number of parents indicated that they wanted to know more about what level of physical intimacy between parents and children is acceptable.

Parents are not fully aware of their child's needs regarding cuddling. Whereas more than half of the children (n = 18) indicated that they often felt the need to cuddle with (one of) their parents, only seven parents reported that their child often wanted to do so. Either not all children express this need actively, or the parents miss the signals of the child in this respect.

Another discrepancy is the fact that, according to the parents, more children have had experience with being in love than children report themselves (Table 2). The parents conclude their children's experience from behaviors they observe: blushing, talking about a certain child very much, showing off.

Parents were also asked whether they knew which parts of their

TABLE 2. Children's experience with being in love, according to parents and children (in n)

	parents	children
yes	23	18
no	6	13
don't know	1	0

body their children regarded as pleasant or exciting. This was difficult for a lot of the parents: one-third (n = 11) couldn't name pleasant body parts of their child and half (n = 14) couldn't name exciting parts. Those parents who could produce answers to these questions mentioned the same body parts as the children did.

Evaluation of the Research Method

The third purpose of our study was to test the research method with regard to its feasibility and usefulness with young children. In our study it was possible to talk directly with relatively young children about what are generally considered to be sensitive topics. It is important to choose the topics and phrase the questions in a way which stays close to children's own level of experience. For example: the term *exciting* body parts proved to be too difficult for quite a few children. Furthermore, questions like 'How does it feel when you cuddle?' elicit more response then questions like 'What does cuddling mean to you?' Since 8- and 9-year old children just start what Piaget calls the phase of concrete operational thinking, they can answer questions easier which relate to concrete experiences than they can elaborate on more abstract questions. It is interesting, however, that some of these children were already quite capable of reflecting on certain situations and the roles of themselves and others in those situations. On the other hand, the information most children give is very fragmented and has little depth. Possibilities for content analysis are limited.

Open questions work quite well with young children. Given their intellectual level, they are hampered less than older children and adults by the phenomenon of 'inference' (deduce what the situation must have been like) and given the opportunity of free reproduction they give rather factual descriptions of certain situations.

The combination of activities (being interviewed, drawing, talking about pictures) helped the children to stay concentrated. However, some 20 minutes really seemed the maximum time the children could stay focused in the interview.

DISCUSSION

It is obvious that physical intimacy means a great deal to these 8- and 9-year old boys and girls. Almost all children like to cuddle, most of them said they often wanted to cuddle with (one of) their parents. Nevertheless, some children stated this never happens. Another part of the children said they only cuddled with toys or animals, but never with people. Either parents underestimate their child's need for cuddling, or children underestimate the amount of physical contact between them and their parents. In general, parents presented a more positive and permissive view of the situation at home with regard to physical intimacy than the children did: more romping, more cuddling, more bathing together. Children may sketch a less positive situation because they feel shame or embarrassment about these subjects. Even though the actual situation at home may be somewhat different, parents obviously regard being open, warm and permissive as the standard with regard to sex education and family relationships.

There are both similarities and differences between children's sexuality as presented in this study and adolescent or adult sexuality. It seems that the sensations and behaviors which accompany the feeling of being in love don't change very much over the years. The confusion and uncertainty which the children describe is similar to the state of mind adolescents and adults are usually in when they're in love. Also the body sensations, like blushing and tickling, are easily recognizable. Furthermore the combination of being in love with fantasizing is common in both children and older people.

Another similarity between children and adolescents is the way in which the sexual development process seems to take place. What is obvious from the interviews with these 8- and 9-year old children is that also in this younger age group different phases of development can be distinguished. There is a big difference between the children who don't yet have an active interest and own experiences in this area, and the children who do. The transition from one phase to the second is presumably stimulated by their cognitive ability to reflect on their own behavior. From this moment on sexual development more and more becomes an active social learning process, whereas experiences at a younger age are incorporated on a more intuitive and basic level.

A difference between children and adolescents and adults is that while older people seem to focus their sexual interest and behavior on specific body parts, such as bottom and genitals, children seem to have a less differentiated awareness of their body. Both with romping and cuddling they use their whole body, and sensations they feel are not limited to sexual parts. We do know, from other studies, that young children have interest in each other's private parts. Probably, this is caused more by the fact that these are indeed parts which are not usually shown in public, and of which children sense that adults consider them special, than that this interest is the result of their own specific and personal sexual motivation.

As with all research, and especially qualitative studies, questions about validity and reliability have to be raised. Are the answers from the children valid, do they reflect the real situation regarding (aspects of) their sexuality? The small sample size makes it impossible to generalize to the total population of 8- and 9-year old boys and girls, but this study gives some interesting directions for further research.

The differences between the answers of parents and children are an important topic with respect to the validity of the information. Instead of discussing which percentage reflects the 'true' situation in these families, it is important to acknowledge the fact that there are two different perspectives at work here. When one is really interested in (aspects of) children's sexuality from the child's perspective one should also talk to children themselves. However, one should realise that the answers of the children are not necessarily a more accurate reflection of the reality. The active involvement of the researcher in the interview situation could steer the behavior of the child in a certain direction. Children are more impressionable than adults, and social desirability is an important issue. To improve the reliability of the material triangulation (the combination of multiple sources and multiple methods of data collection) has been used in this study. Within the interview situation, some themes were discussed more than once, so inconsistencies could be discovered and discussed. In the original report (Laan 1994) an elaborate methodological account is given, which gives insight into the choices the research team has made, their reasons for doing so, and in the way the interviews with the children were conducted. Though a qualitative study can never be totally copied by the next researcher, replication of (parts of) this study is certainly possible.

REFERENCES

Bancroft J. (1989). *Human sexuality and its problems*. Edinburgh: Churchill Livingstone.
Constantine L., Martinson F. (1981). *Children and sex; new findings, new perspectives*. Little, Brown and Company, Boston.
Frayser S. (1995). "Defining Childhood Sexuality: An Anthropological Approach," in *Annals of Sex Research*.
Laan M. (1994). *Kinderen en hun beleving van lichamelijkheid*. Doctoraalscriptie Universiteit van Amsterdam/NISSO.
Laan M., Rademakers J., Straver C. (1996). "De beleving van lichamelijkheid en intimiteit door kinderen," in *Kind en Adolescent*; 17, 1, 32-37
Rademakers J., Straver C. (1986). *Van fascinatie naar relatie*. NISSO, Zeist.
Rademakers J., Laan M., Straver C. (1995). *Studying children's sexuality from the child's perspective*; presentation at the 21 Annual Meeting of the International Academy of Sex Research in Provincetown (Mass.), USA.
Sandfort T. (1989). *Seksuele ervaringen van kinderen; betekenis en effect voor later*. Van Loghum Slaterus, Deventer.
Vogels T., Van der Vliet R. (1990). *Jeugd en Seks*, SDU, Den Haag.
Zanden I. van der (1992). Sexueel gedrag van kinderen: een literatuuroverzicht. *Tijdschrift voor ontwikkelingspsychologie*; 19, 133-153.

The Association of Sexual Behavior
with Externalizing Behaviors
in a Community Sample
of Prepubertal Children

Heino F. L. Meyer-Bahlburg, Dr. rer. nat.
Curtis Dolezal, PhD
David E. Sandberg, PhD

Heino F. L. Meyer-Bahlburg and Curtis Dolezal are affiliated with HIV Center for Clinical and Behavioral Studies, New York State Psychiatric Institute, and Department of Psychiatry, College of Physicians & Surgeons, Columbia University. David E. Sandberg, is affiliated with Division of Child and Adolescent Psychiatry, Children's Hospital of Buffalo, and Departments of Psychiatry and Pediatrics, State University of New York at Buffalo, NY.

Address correspondence to Heino F. L. Meyer-Bahlburg, NYSPI Unit 10, 722 West 168th Street, New York, NY 10032 (e-mail address: meyerb@child.cpmc. columbia.edu).

We thank the participating mothers for their cooperation. Patricia Connolly provided word-processing assistance.

This research was supported in part by the National Research Service Award HDO6726 from NICHD to David Sandberg, by a Small Grant from the Spencer Foundation, Grant 87-0982-84 from the William T. Grant Foundation, and a grant from the Ford Foundation to Anke Ehrhardt and Heino Meyer-Bahlburg, by NIMH Clinical Research Grant MH-30906 to Donald Klein, and by NIMH Center Grant 2-P50-MH43520 to Anke Ehrhardt.

A preliminary report of the data was presented as a poster at the 21st Annual Meeting of the International Academy of Sex Research, Provincetown, MA, September 20-24, 1995.

[Haworth co-indexing entry note]: "The Association of Sexual Behavior with Externalizing Behaviors in a Community Sample of Perpubertal Children." Meyer-Bahlburg, Heino F. L., Curtis Dolezal, and David E. Sandberg. Co-published simultaneously in *Journal of Psychology & Human Sexuality* (The Haworth Press, Inc.) Vol. 12, No. 1/2, 2000, pp. 61-79; and: *Childhood Sexuality: Normal Sexual Behavior and Development* (ed: Theo G.M. Sandfort, and Jany Rademakers) The Haworth Press, Inc., 2000, pp. 61-79. Single or multiple copies of this article are available for a fee from The Haworth Document Delivery Service [1-800-342-9678, 9:00 a.m. - 5:00 p.m. (EST). E-mail address: getinfo@haworthpressinc.com].

ABSTRACT. On the basis of the problem-behavior theory for adolescence, we hypothesized that already during childhood sexual behavior is associated with (non-sexual) externalizing behaviors and tested the hypothesis in a community sample. In the context of a postal questionnaire survey of 6-10 year old children, the parents of 349 girls and 326 boys completed the Child Behavior Checklist (CBCL). The CBCL Sex Problems scale did not differ between genders, ethnic groups, or age groups. For both girls and boys, the scores on the Sex Problems scale correlated significantly but modestly (maximum r = 0.35) with all other CBCL scales; only in boys did the correlations with externalizing behaviors exceed those with other scales. We conclude that children from a community sample who show sexual behavior as defined by the CBCL tend to be the ones with increased behavioral/emotional problems in general, with only modest specificity in symptomatology. *[Article copies available for a fee from The Haworth Document Delivery Service: 1-800-342-9678. E-mail address: <getinfo@haworthpressinc.com> Website: <http://www.HaworthPress.com>]*

KEYWORDS. Child Behavior Checklist, CBCL, sexual behavior in childhood, problem behavior therapy

INTRODUCTION

In contrast to other areas of child development, research on childhood sexual behavior is underdeveloped. The existing data come mainly from studies that investigate childhood sexual behavior as a function of one of four factors: (1) age, (2) pubertal maturation, (3) sexual abuse, and (4) "problem behaviors" in general.

Descriptive studies of childhood sexuality try to answer the questions, what types of sexual behaviors are typical or common for a given age (or, sometimes, developmental stage), or at what ages they emerge. Most of the available data have been collected retrospectively from adults or older adolescents to cover the early adolescent and sometimes childhood years (e.g., Kinsey, Pomeroy, & Martin, 1948; Kinsey, Pomeroy, Martin, & Gebhard, 1953; Rotheram-Borus et al., 1992a, 1992b; Rosario, Meyer-Bahlburg, Hunter, Exner, Gwadz, & Keller, 1996). Studies of concurrent sexual behavior have usually been limited to surveys of mid- or older adolescents. Most of the few sexuality studies available on children of elementary school age use parents as informants (e.g., Achenbach & Edelbrock, 1983; Achenbach, 1991; Friedrich, Grambsch, Broughton, Kuiper, & Beilke, 1991), and only very few studies have attempted to obtain information from prepubertal children directly (e.g., Broderick, 1966; Elias & Gebhard, 1969; Paikoff, 1995; Stanton et al., 1994).

The second factor, sexual maturation, is of obvious developmental relevance. There is now a considerable body of empirical data linking the development of sexuality to the timing of puberty, to pubertal stage, or to systemic sex hormone levels (Meyer-Bahlburg, 1980; Rodgers & Rowe, 1993; Udry, 1994).

Research on child sexual abuse tends to assess sexuality in children more directly, albeit in a clinical subgroup. Despite methodological limitations (e.g., the prevailing retrospective approach and the limited representativeness of most samples), the data indicate that sexual initiation of prepubertal children by adolescents or adults tends to sexualize the children; i.e., they show an increased frequency of behaviors such as masturbation, putting objects into the vagina or anus, age-inappropriate or precocious sexual knowledge, sexual play with dolls, seductive behavior, requesting sexual stimulation (Mian, Wehrspann, Klajner-Diamond, LeBaron, & Winder, 1986; Cosentino, Meyer-Bahlburg, Alpert, Weinberg, & Gaines, 1995). It is difficult, however, to disentangle the sexual from the psychiatric sequelae of sexual abuse, and the effects of sexual abuse from the effects of concurrent physical abuse or a disturbed home environment in general (Beitchman, Zucker, Hood, DaCosta, & Akman, 1991; Browne & Finkelhor, 1986).

Finally, in the psychosocial study of adolescents, early onset of sexual intercourse and an increased number of sexual partners have been associated with the emergence of other "problem behaviors" such as smoking, alcohol and drug use, delinquency, and disruptive behavior (Jessor & Jessor, 1977; Gottfredson & Hirschi, 1990, 1994; Ketterlinus, Lamb, & Nitz, 1994; Rodgers & Rowe, 1990). From a clinical perspective, such "problem behaviors" have much in common with the behaviors subsumed under the diagnostic category of conduct disorder (and, by implication, antisocial personality disorder), and an association of conduct disorder with certain features of sexual behavior has long been recognized. For instance, "has forced someone into sexual activity" is one of the (non-obligatory) criteria of the diagnosis of conduct disorder (American Psychiatric Association, 1994, p. 90); as associated features are listed, for both genders, an early onset of sexual behavior, and, for females, prostitution (p. 87-88). The empirical basis for the association of sexual behavior with (non-sexual) conduct-disorder related behaviors has been provided by a number of wide-ranging investigations of clinical and non-clinical populations (e.g., Jessor & Jessor, 1977; Robins, 1966; see also Ensminger, 1987). Also, studies of adolescent sex offenders in general (e.g., Becker, Kaplan, Cunningham-Rathner, & Kavoussi, 1986; Davis & Leitenberg, 1987; Kavoussi, Kaplan, & Becker, 1988) and young male prostitutes in particular (e.g., Pleak & Meyer-Bahlburg, 1990) have found increased rates of conduct disorder in their psychiatric histories. However, the strength of the overall association between non-sexual conduct problems and sexual behavior is only moderate. That is, many persons with conduct disorder do not meet the sexual criteria, and many others with unusually early onset of sexual behavior show no other problem behaviors (Ensminger, 1990).

The association of some aspects of adolescent sex behavior with a cluster of non-sexual problem behaviors raises the question at what stage of development the association originates and by what mechanism. There has been a large amount of research on the development of (non-sexual) conduct-disorder related behaviors, demonstrating their roots in early childhood, their dependence on parent-child interaction patterns at that time, and their remarkable long-term stability (e.g., Kellam, 1990; Loeber, 1990; Patterson, 1982; Snyder & Patterson, 1995). Given that children of elementary-school age engage in a certain amount of sexual behavior, it is conceivable that at least some of it is associated with non-sexual conduct-disorder related behaviors at that age already. Such an early association is, in fact, suggested by clinical observations (see, for instance, the categorization of childhood sexual behaviors provided by Gil & Johnson, 1993, pp. 41-51). Whether at elementary-school age some aspects of sexual behavior are just an integral part of a complex problem-behavior trait such as "low self-control" (Gottfredson & Hirschi, 1990, 1994), or whether there are certain demographic, family, psychosocial, and contextual factors that more specifically determine those aspects of sexual behavior is yet to be investigated.

Several factors have made the study of childhood sexuality and its determinants an urgent matter. For instance, it is well known that over the course of this century the onset of peno-vaginal intercourse has moved to significantly earlier ages (Hofferth, 1990), and the corresponding issues of premarital sex and teenage pregnancy have been of public concern for decades. With the recent expansion of STD- and HIV-related research on sexual behavior, we have become increasingly aware that all penetrative sexual practices, i.e., peno-vaginal, oral-genital, or penile-anal intercourse, pose risks of variable degrees of infection with sexually transmitted diseases (STD) in general, and with the human immunodeficiency virus (HIV) in particular. It has also become clear that significant numbers of girls, and, more so, of boys, begin such activities during early puberty or even earlier (e.g., Zelnik & Shah, 1983; Rotheram-Borus et al., 1992 a, b; Rosario et al., 1996). Thus, not only childhood conditions as antecedents of adolescent sex behavior, but childhood sexual behavior itself has become a matter of public health concerns. Consequently, and in analogy to what has emerged for the area of conduct disorder, the introduction of STD- and HIV-preventive efforts before adolescence needs to be seriously considered.

It is in this context that we have begun a series of projects on sexual behavior in childhood. As a first step, we wanted to analyze recently collected data sets for the hypothesized association of sexual behavior with conduct-disorder related behaviors. The pertinent variables available in these data sets were the various scales of the Child Behavior Checklist (CBCL; Achenbach & Edelbrock, 1983; Achenbach, 1991). Thus, sexual behavior was operationalized as the CBCL Sex Problems scale and conduct disorder as the Externalizing scale (which overlaps with, but is narrower in scope than "problem behavior" as defined by the Jessors and their followers). In the first study (Meyer-Bahlburg, Dolezal, Wasserman, & Jaramillo, in press), we evaluated a sample of boys aged 5-11 years who were at increased risk for the development of conduct-disorder related behaviors in general because they were the younger brothers of adolescent boys who had been adjudicated by family courts in New York City. Our results showed that these high-risk boys received higher sores on both the Sex Problems scale and the scales of non-sexual behavioral/emotional problems of the CBCL (Achenbach, 1991) than Achenbach's non-clinical norm sample. Sexual behavior as operationalized here was, indeed, significantly related to Achenbach's Externalizing scale and its component syndrome scales, but also to the Internalizing scale and its component scales; i.e., the relationship was not specific to conduct-disorder related behaviors.

The purpose of the current paper is to analyze analogous data for a less highly specialized sample, namely, a community sample which by its nature permits a wider generalization. As the sample includes both boys and girls, it also permits a gender comparison.

METHOD

Sample

The English-speaking parents of all boys and girls age 6-10 years in an ethnically and demographically heterogeneous school district were invited to participate in a postal survey including several questionnaires. The only exclusion criterium was the absence of an English-speaking parent/guardian living in the home. The survey was conducted over the two academic years, 1986-88. Recruitment involved an initial contact letter and multiple phone follow-ups or home visits as necessary. Details of the procedures have been described elsewhere (Sandberg, Meyer-Bahlburg, & Yager, 1991; Sandberg, Meyer-Bahlburg, Ehrhardt, & Yager, 1993). Usable questionnaire sets were received for 72% of the eligible sample. The demographics are listed on Table 1.

Assessment

The questionnaire battery included the Child Behavior Checklist (CBCL; Achenbach & Edelbrock, 1983; Achenbach, 1991), an extensively standardized parent-report questionnaire designed to obtain standardized descriptions of a child's behavior as the parent sees it

TABLE 1. Sample Characteristics

	Boys N = 326	Girls N = 349
Ethnicity (%)		
African-American	33.4	40.4
Latino	14.1	13.2
White	43.3	39.0
Other	9.2	7.4
Age (years):		
Range	6-10	6-10
Mean	8.43	8.57
School Grade[a] (Mean)	2.29	2.51
Parental Education[b]		
Mean	4.74	4.74

[a]Kindergarten coded 0. One child not in school and six in special classes were treated as missing data.
[b]Hollingshead (1975), 7-point scale; 4 = High School graduate, 5 = partial college or specialized training.

(Achenbach, 1991, p. iii). According to the 1991 manual, the first part of the CBCL assesses social competencies and the second behavioral/ emotional problems. This article is concerned with the second part only. The "problem items" of the second part are formulated as observational statements that vary in the degree to which a "problem" is implied (e.g., #108 "Wets the bed"; #22 "Disobedient at home"; #52 "Feels too guilty"). For each item, the parent is to mark whether the item is "very true or often true" (response score: 2) of the child, "sometimes or somewhat true" (1), or "not true" (0); the time frame is "now or within the past 6 months." In the 1991 edition whose norms were used here, the problem items are the basis for a variety of scales (listed on Table 4). Eight syndrome scales were derived by principal components analyses of the problem items and orthogonal (varimax) rotation. An additional Sex Problems scale (its six items are listed on Table 3) was derived by the same principal-components analyses among 4-5 and 6-11 year old children, but not among adolescents. Subsets of the 8 syndrome scales were combined into an Internalizing scale (including the syndrome scales, Withdrawn, Somatic Complaints, Anxious/Depressed), and an Externalizing scale (including the syndrome scales, Delinquent Behavior, Aggressive Behavior), respectively, based on the results of secondary (principal axis) factor analyses. Responses summed up over all problem items (including those that are not captured by the syndrome scales and the Sex Problems scale) yield a Total problem score. To facilitate clinical interpretation, Achenbach (1991) defined cut-off scores of a clinical range in terms of statistical distribution criteria for all scales except the Sex Problems scale (see Table 4, footnote).

It is important to note that the CBCL terms used by Achenbach are conceptually not strictly defined and lend themselves easily to misinterpretations from various perspectives. Achenbach refers to the content of the items as "behavioral/emotional problems." However, as we know from routine clinical inquiry about the CBCL, a parent who marks an item as 1 or 2 agrees to a behavioral description which s/he does not necessarily perceive as a "problem." Similarly, in using the CBCL, particularly the Sex Problems scale, and adopting the terminology of Achenbach's manual, we do not consider the behaviors captured by the individual items or their aggregation necessarily as "problems" or as "psychopathology." Achenbach's term "problem" is also not intended to be identical with "problem behavior" as used by Jessor and Jessor and their followers. The term "syndrome" used by Achenbach suggests equivalence with the categories "syndrome" or "disorder" as used in medicine and psychiatry, but the underlying conceptualizations are not identical. A "clinical range" denotes a relatively uncommon more extreme range of behavior, but the statistical definition by itself does not create equivalence with the clinical concept of a syndrome. (See Rutter, Harrington, Quinton, & Pickles, 1994, for a concise overview of the conceptual distinction between dimensional and categorical formulations of clinical disorders.) On the other hand, we are well aware that high scores on any one of the CBCL scales, including on the Sex Problems scale, are associated with an increased likelihood that the child meets criteria for a clinical disorder or that the family will benefit from some form of mental-health intervention.

Data Analysis

The relationship of the Sex Problems scale with the other CBCL scales of behavioral/emotional problems and the influence of demographic variables is the focus of the present report. Using the scales and norms of Achenbach (1991), we employed simple group-comparison statistics and correlational analysis. For specific additional issues, standard multivariate procedures such as regression analysis and factor analysis were used. As recommended by Achenbach (1991, p. 190), all statistical analyses were based on raw scores rather than T-scores.

RESULTS

Demographic and Background Variables

The total sample included 331 boys and 354 girls; for 5 boys and 5 girls, the CBCL questionnaires had to be excluded from analysis because they had more than 8 problem items missing (not counting items 2, 4, 56h, 113, as per Achenbach, 1991, p. 249). As Table 1 shows, about two-fifths of the sample were White, over a third was African-American, one-sixth Latino, and the remainder Asian and other ethnic groups. The children were relatively evenly distributed over the age range of 6-10 years, with a mean of 8 1/2 years. The average school grade was third. Mean parental education level was between high school graduate and partial college or specialized training.

Sexual Behavior Compared to Norms

The first question we wanted to answer was how our community sample compared to Achenbach's (1991) norms. For 52 out of 326 boys (16.0%) and for 46 out of 349 girls (13.2%), the parent/guardian marked at least one sex item on the Sex Problems scale as 1 or 2 (as compared to 17% of our high-risk boys). As Table 2 shows, the scale means of both boys and girls were significantly lower than those in the clinically-referred norm samples of Achenbach (1991); the community girls were comparable to the non-referred norm girls, while the community boys were slightly, but significantly higher than the non-referred norm boys. Boys and girls did not differ in the Sexual Problems scale mean, nor on individual items, except that boys were significantly higher (p = .01) on the item, "Thinks About Sex Too Much" (Table 3).

Association of Sexual Behavior with Demographic Variables

Scores on the Sex Problems scale were not significantly associated with age (for boys, r = −.05; for girls, r = −.00) nor with ethnicity. The Sex Problems scale was significantly associated with Parental Education among boys (r = −.13, p = .018), but not among girls (r = −.01).

Non-Sexual Behaviors Compared to Norms

Comparing our non-sexual data to the respective Achenbach (1991) norms, we found that the means of the current samples on most CBCL scales were significantly but only slightly higher than those of the clinically non-referred norm samples; yet, they were significantly and markedly lower than those of the clinically referred norm samples (not shown). The proportion of our children scoring in the clinical range on the CBCL scales was elevated compared to Achenbach (1991) non-referred norms (Table 4).

Association of the Sex Problems Scale with Other CBCL Scales

Our primary question was whether the Sex Problems scale was correlated with the Externalizing scale or its component syndrome

TABLE 2. Sex Problems scale means of present samples versus norm samples

| | Sex Problems | | t-test |
	Mean	S.D.	p
1. Boys			
Present sample (N = 326)	0.2	0.7	
Achenbach[a] non-referred			
sample (N = 582)	0.1	0.5	.013
Achenbach[a] referred			
sample (N = 582)	0.5	1.1	< .001
2. Girls			
Present sample (N = 349)	0.2	0.6	
Achenbach[b] non-referred			
sample (N = 619)	0.2	0.5	1.000
Achenbach[b] referred			
sample (N = 619)	0.6	1.2	< .001

[a]Achenbach (1991), p. 252
[b]Achenbach (1991), p. 254

TABLE 3. Number of children scoring on individual Sex Problems scale items

Items	Boys (N = 326)			Girls (N = 349)		
	0	1	2	0	1	2
5. Behaves like opposite sex	311	11	4	330	16	3
59. Plays with own sex parts in public	312	14	0	339	7	3
60. Plays with own sex parts too much	316	9	1	335	12	2
73. Sexual problems[a]	326	0	0	348	0	0
96. Thinks about sex too much[b]	301	19	6	335	11	1
110. Wishes to be of opposite sex[c,d]	320	3	0	338	8	0

Number with missing data in girls: [a]1, [b]2, [c]3; in boys: [d]3.

scales, and secondarily whether there were also correlations with other syndrome scales. As Table 5 shows, the linear correlations of the Sex Problems scale with all other CBCL scales were significant. Of the children for whom the parents marked at least one sex item as 1 or 2, the majority (excluding those who fell right on the median score) had

TABLE 4. Number of children in clinical range on CBCL scales, with binomial tests[a]

CBCL scales	Boys (N = 326)			Girls (N = 349)		
	N	%	1-tailed p	N	%	1-tailed p
Withdrawn	11	3.4	.058	6	1.7	.427
Somatic complaints	10	3.1	.119	12	3.4	.042
Anxious/depressed	16	4.9	< .001	15	4.3	.002
Social problems	9	2.8	.217	31	8.9	< .001
Thought problems	1	0.3	.024[b]	1	0.3	.018[b]
Attention problems	13	4.0	.009	22	6.3	< .001
Delinquent behavior	17	5.2	< .001	20	5.7	< .001
Aggressive behavior	11	3.4	.058	17	4.9	< .001
Internalizing	65	19.9	< .001	48	13.8	< .001
Externalizing	51	15.6	< .001	56	16.0	< .001
Total score	65	19.9	< .001	68	19.5	< .001

[a]Comparing observed proportion in clinical range to expected proportion of 2% for individual scales and 9% for Internalizing, Externalizing, and Total score.
[b]Direction against expectations.

TABLE 5. Pearson correlations of Sex Problems scale with other CBCL scales (raw scores)

CBCL scales	Boys (N = 326)		Girls (N = 349)	
	r	p	r	p
Withdrawn	.13	.024	.26	< .001
Somatic complaints	.12	.036	.16	.003
Anxious/depressed	.18	.001	.27	< .001
Social problems	.20	< .001	.21	< .001
Thought problems	.19	< .001	.15	.004
Attention problems	.22	< .001	.33	< .001
Delinquent behavior[a]	.29	< .001	.22	< .001
Aggressive behavior	.33	< .001	.33	< .001
Internalizing	.18	.001	.29	< .001
Externalizing[a]	.34	< .001	.32	< .001
Total score[b]	.30	< .001	.35	< .001

[a]One item also in the Sex Problem scale (Thinks about sex too much) has been removed from the Delinquent Behavior and Externalizing scales.
[b]After exclusion of the six items of the Sex Problems scale.

scores above the sample median on most of the other CBCL scales, significantly different from the other children (not shown). In our sample of high-risk boys (Meyer-Bahlburg et al., in press), we had found many curvilinear relationships between the Sex Problems scale and the other CBCL scales, with particularly high Sex Problems scores in boys who scored high on the syndrome scales. For the current samples only one quadratic regression component was conventionally significant: for Withdrawn in Boys, p = .025; three were marginal: Withdrawn in Girls, p = .056; Attention Problems in Boys, p = .059; Delinquent Behavior in Boys, p = .077 (none shown). For the boys, the Sex Problems scale correlated significantly higher with the Externalizing scale than with the Internalizing scale (Chi-square = 4.78, p ≤ 0.029), and higher with its two component scales, Aggressive Behavior and Delinquent Behavior, than with the component syndrome scales of the Internalizing scale (although the difference was not statistically significant for Anxious/Depressed). However, for the girls, there was no similarly salient pattern, mostly because the correlations of the Sex Problems scale with the Internalizing scale and its components were not as low as in the boys.

Decomposition of the Sex Problems Scale

Conceptually, the Sex Problems scale combines two categories of items, namely two gender-related items depicting cross-gender behavior (#5 and #110) and four items that more specifically assess sexual behavior. In Achenbach's principal-component analyses of all problem items for children 4-5 and 6-11 years of age (all referred for mental-health services), the Sex Problems syndrome emerged as one dimension (Achenbach, 1991, pp. 39-40). However, in our data set, when we subjected the 6 items by themselves to principal axis factor analyses (after removal of the item, "Sex Problems," which was scored 0 for all children), the sex items separated from the gender items for the total sample (both unrotated and rotated solutions) and for the girls alone (unrotated solution only), but not for the boys alone (Table 6). (Principal axis factor analysis avoids the exaggeration of factor loadings typical of principal components analysis, especially in the case of a small number of items [Snook & Gorsuch, 1989].) The correspondingly derived 3-item (or 4-item) Sex scale and the 2-item Gender scale intercorrelated r = .22 (p < .001) in boys and r = .08 (p = .161) in girls. The pattern of correlations of the 3-item Sex scale with the other CBCL scales (Table 7) was very similar to that of the 6-item Sex Problems scale. In contrast, the correlations of the 2-item Gender scale with the other CBCL scales were generally much lower and less distinctly patterned (Table 7).

TABLE 6. Factor analyses (principal axis) of the Sex Problems items (raw scores), rotated factor matrices

	Total sample (N = 667)	
	FACTOR 1	FACTOR 2
ITEM 59	.64	− .02
ITEM 60	.60	.15
ITEM 96	.14	.11
ITEM 5	.13	.69
ITEM 110	.02	.26
	Boys only (N = 323)	
	FACTOR 1	FACTOR 2
ITEM 60	.82	− .07
ITEM 59	.52	.18
ITEM 5	.36	.11
ITEM 96	.16	− .01
ITEM 110	.04	.62
	Girls only (N = 344)	
	FACTOR 1	FACTOR 2
ITEM 59	.68	− .07
ITEM 60	.54	.13
ITEM 5	.03	.64
ITEM 110	.01	.40
ITEM 96	.15	.17

Note: The slightly reduced N's are due to listwise deletion of cases with missing data. Items 59, 60, 96 are sex behavior items; items 5 and 110 are gender items. Item 73 was excluded because all children scored 0. For item wording, see Table 3.

DISCUSSION

Our main findings can be summarized as follows: (1) Among 6-10-year-old children from a community sample, approximately 1 in 6 boys and 1 in 7 girls showed sexual behavior as reported by their parents on the CBCL. (2) An association of sexual behavior with externalizing behaviors exists already in middle childhood, but does not appear to be exclusive, i.e., there are significant relationships with other CBCL scales as well. However, at least in boys, the association with externalizing behaviors is highest. (3) The associations of sexual behavior with non-sexual CBCL scales seen here in boys and girls from a community sample are similar to (albeit somewhat weaker than) those shown by high-risk boys. (4) Removing the gender items from the Sex Problems scale does not increase the specificity of the

TABLE 7. Pearson correlations of the 4-item Sex scale and the Gender scale with other CBCL scales (raw scores)

| CBCL Scales | Sex Scale | | | | Gender Scale | | | |
| | Boys (N = 326) | | Girls (N = 349) | | Boys (N = 326) | | Girls (N = 349) | |
	r	p	r	p	r	p	r	p
Withdrawn	.12	.035	.30	< .001	.07	.210	.05	.351
Somatic complaints	.12	.037	.19	< .001	.05	.352	.04	.439
Anxious/depressed	.21	< .001	.29	< .001	.04	.469	.08	.148
Social problems	.23	< .001	.20	< .001	.04	.421	.09	.092
Thought problems	.18	.002	.11	.040	.13	.015	.11	.036
Attention problems	.22	< .001	.30	< .001	.09	.087	.17	.001
Delinquent behavior[a]	.28	< .001	.20	< .001	.14	.011	.12	.031
Aggressive behavior	.35	< .001	.28	< .001	.11	.040	.20	< .001
Internalizing	.19	.001	.32	< .001	.06	.265	.07	.169
Externalizing[a]	.36	< .001	.28	< .001	.13	.021	.19	< .001
Total score[b]	.32	< .001	.33	< .001	.11	.048	.16	.002

[a]One item which is also in the Sex scale (thinks about sex too much) has been removed from the Delinquent Behavior and Externalizing scales.
[b]Minus the four items of the Sex scale (for the correlation of Total score and Sex scale); minus the two items of the Gender scale (for the correlation of Total score and Gender scale).

pattern of correlations of the set of the remaining four sex items with other CBCL scales.

It is not surprising that the means of most CBCL scales in the current samples were higher than Achenbach's (1991) norms for non-referred children. Unlike Achenbach, we did not exclude from our community sample those children who had been referred to mental-health or educational services for psychiatric or learning problems (see also Sandberg et al., 1991). Thus, the fact that our sample falls in between Achenbach's non-referred and referred samples is entirely in line with expectations.

Our study yielded an association of sexual behavior with diverse non-sexual CBCL scales of behavioral/emotional problems. Only for boys were the correlations with externalizing behaviors particularly salient. Thus, our data suggest that the association of early onset of sexual intercourse and non-sexual problem behaviors described for adolescents by Jessor and Jessor (1977) and others may have a child-hood precursor, at least in boys from a community sample. However, we had not seen such a correlation pattern in our previous analysis of data from high-risk boys (Meyer-Bahlburg et al., in press). On the other hand, Friedrich et al. (1991) reported findings similar to the ones we report here, namely higher correlations of his Child Sexual Behavior Inventory with the CBCL Externalizing scale than the Internalizing scale in both boys and girls from a community sample of children age 2-12 years, but the differences were very slight and not statistically significant. (The correlations with the component syndrome scales were not provided.) Finally, if one analyses the data contained in Achenbach's (1991, p. 256, 258) intercorrelation tables, a similar pattern is suggested by his girls' data, but not by his boys' data. Unfortunately, Achenbach's correlations are based on T-scores whose construction involved truncations of raw-score distributions. In addition, Achenbach's norm samples of non-referred children are not comparable to community samples as ordinarily defined, but exclude all children who were referred to mental-health or educational services. Thus, Achenbach's data are not directly comparable to ours, and their interpretation is more problematic. In combination, the existing data for community samples suggest a moderate association of parent-reported child sexual behavior with non-sexual behavior/emotional problems, with only a minor salience of externalizing behavior patterns in this association.

The modest degree of specificity seen in our correlation patterns may reflect, at least in part, two limitations of this study. One is the assessment instrument available. The Sex Problems scale is a very brief and superficial screen of sexual behavior in childhood. Moreover, in its original form, the scale combines sex and (cross-) gender items. Cross-gender behavior, when severe enough to meet criteria for gender identity disorder, is associated more with internalizing than externalizing symptoms, at least in boys (Zucker & Bradley, 1995, ch. 5). Thus, the inclusion of cross-gender items in the Sex Problems scale might make it harder to find a specific association of the scale with externalizing behavior. An additional problem is the content of the four sex items themselves. Two of them deal with masturbation, the others are relatively global. By contrast, the aspects of sexual behavior included in the problem behavior theory involve partner sex, not self-masturbation. Also, two of the sex-behavior items (# 60 and # 96) tend to present "problem" statements rather than plain behavioral descriptions. That is, the parents do not endorse whether or not a specific behavior occurs, but whether it is a problem ("too much"). Clinical experience has taught us that parents vary tremendously in their sensitivity to childhood behaviors; thus, these items are bound to reflect, in part, parents' evaluation of their children's behavior as problematic rather than just behavior observations. And it would be plausible to assume that the problem perspective also increases the communality of the ratings of the sex items with those from other behavioral domains whose formulations also reflect a problem perspective, thereby lessening the specificity of associations.

Finally, there is the problem of the information available to the parent. We know from clinical experience that the parents see or hear about only some of the sexual behavior of their children, and probably less the older the children are. Thus, assessment of the sexual behavior of children directly is highly desirable if we are to make faster progress in our understanding of childhood sexuality. For logistic and ethical reasons, such assessments of children of elementary-school age cannot be done by observation, but are limited to self-report, usually elicited by interview. Unfortunately, children pose more of a challenge for sexual interviewing than adolescents and adults do (O'Sullivan, Meyer-Bahlburg, & Wasserman, this issue), and standard survey methods for the detailed assessment of childhood sexuality are yet to be developed.

Apart from the assessment issues, there is another factor that may make it more difficult to find a specific association between sexual and externalizing behaviors, namely the comparatively young age of the children in our samples. The usual studies of this association are conducted in adolescents and adults in whom both sexual behaviors and non-sexual behavioral/emotional problems are more differentiated and can, therefore, be assessed with more specificity than at the age of our sample.

As found by other researchers (e.g., Ensminger, 1990) in adolescents, our data also indicate that by no means all children with general behavioral/emotional problems, nor even all those with problems of externalizing character, show sexual behavior. Which risk factors or predictors distinguish problem-behavior children for whom the parents report sexual behavior from the others without is yet to be mapped out.

REFERENCES

Achenbach, T.M. (1991). *Manual for the Child Behavior Checklist/4-18 and 1991 Profile*. Burlington, VT: University of Vermont Department of Psychiatry.

Achenbach, T.M., & Edelbrock, C.S. (1983). *Manual for the Child Behavior Checklist and Revised Child Behavior Profile*. Burlington, VT: University of Vermont Department of Psychiatry.

American Psychiatric Association (1994). *Diagnostic and Statistical Manual of Mental Disorders. Fourth Edition. (DSM-IV)*. Washington, D.C.: American Psychiatric Association.

Becker, J.V., Kaplan, M.S., Cunningham-Rathner, J., & Kavoussi, R. (1986). Characteristics of adolescent incest sexual perpetrators: Preliminary findings. *Journal of Family Violence, 1*, 85-97.

Beitchman, J.H., Zucker, K.J., Hood, J.E..DaCosta, G.A., & Akman, D. (1991). A review of the short-term effects of child sexual abuse. *Child Abuse and Neglect, 15*, 537-556.

Broderick, C.B. (1966). Socio-sexual development in a suburban community. *Journal of Sex Research, 2*, 1-24.

Browne, A., & Finkelhor, D. (1986). Impact of child sexual abuse: A review of the research. *Psychological Bulletin, 99*, 66-77.

Cosentino, C.E., Meyer-Bahlburg, H.F.L., Alpert, J.L., Weinberg, S.L., & Gaines, R. (1995). Sexual behavior problems and psychopathology symptoms in sexually abused girls. *Journal of the American Academy of Child and Adolescent Psychiatry, 34*, 1033-1042.

Davis, G.E., & Leitenberg, H. (1987). Adolescent sex offenders. *Psychological Bulletin, 101*, 417-427.

Elias, J., & Gebhard, P. (1969). Sexuality and sexual learning in childhood. *Phi Delta Kappan, 50*, 401-405.

Ensminger, M.E. (1987). Adolescent sexual behavior as it relates to other transition behaviors in youth. In S.L. Hofferth, & C.D. Hayes (Eds.), *Risking the future. Adolescent sexuality, pregnancy, and childbearing, Vol. II, Working papers and statistical appendixes* (pp. 36-55). Washington, DC: National Academy Press.

Ensminger, M.E. (1990). Sexual activity and problem behaviors among black, urban adolescents. *Child Development, 61*, 2032-2046

Friedrich, W.N., Grambsch, P., Broughton, D., Kuiper, J., & Beilke, R.L. (1991). Normative sexual behavior in children. *Pediatrics, 88*, 456-464.

Gil, E., & Johnson, T.C. (1993). *Sexualized children. Assessment and treatment of sexualized children and children who molest*. Rockville, MD: Launch Press.

Gottfredson, M.R., & Hirschi, T. (1990). *A general theory of crime*. Stanford, CA: Stanford University Press.

Gottfredson, M.R., & Hirschi, T. (1994). A general theory of adolescent problem behavior: Problems and prospects. In R.D. Ketterlinus, & M.E. Lamb (Eds.), *Adolescent problem behaviors. Issues and research* (pp. 41-56). Hillsdale, NJ: Lawrence Erlbaum Associates, Publishers.

Hofferth, S.L. (1990). Trends in adolescent sexual activity, contraception, and pregnancy in the United States. In J. Bancroft, & J.M. Reinisch (Eds.), *Adolescence and puberty* (pp. 217-233). New York: Oxford University Press.

Jessor, R., & Jessor, S.L. (1977). *Problem behavior and psychological development. A longitudinal study of youth*. New York: Academic Press.

Kavoussi, R.J., Kaplan, M., & Becker, J.V. (1988). Psychiatric diagnoses in adolescent sex offenders. *Journal of the American Academy of Child and Adolescent Psychiatry, 27*, 241-243.

Kellam, S.G. (1990). Developmental epidemiologic framework for family research on depression and aggression. In G.R. Patterson (Ed.), *Depression and aggression in family interaction* (pp. 11-48). Englewood Cliffs, NJ: Erlbaum.

Ketterlinus, R.D., Lamb, M.E., & Nitz, K.A. (1994). Adolescent nonsexual and sex-related problem behaviors: Their prevalence, consequences, and co-occurrence. In R.D. Ketterlinus, & M. E. Lamb, *Adolescent problem behaviors. Issues and research* (pp. 17-39). Hillsdale, NJ: Lawrence Erlbaum Associates Publishers.

Kinsey, A.C., Pomeroy, W.B., & Martin, C.E. (1948). *Sexual behavior in the human male*. Philadelphia: W.B. Saunders.

Kinsey, A.C., Pomeroy, W.B., Martin, C.E., & Gebhard, P.H. (1953). *Sexual behavior in the human female*. Philadelphia: W.B. Saunders.

Loeber, R. (1990). Development and risk factors of juvenile antisocial behavior and delinquency. *Clinical Psychology Review, 10*, 1-41.

Meyer-Bahlburg, H.F.L. (1980). Sexuality in early adolescence. In B. Wolman, & J. Money (Eds.), *Handbook of human sexuality* (pp. 60-82). Englewood Cliffs, NJ: Prentice-Hall, Inc.

Meyer-Bahlburg, H.F.L., Dolezal, C., Wasserman, G.A., & Jaramillo, B.M. (in press). Prepubertal boys' sexual behavior. *AIDS Education and Prevention*.

Mian, M., Wehrspann, W., Klajner-Diamond, H., LeBaron, D., & Winder, C. (1986). Review of 125 children 6 years of age and under who were sexually abused. *Child Abuse and Neglect, 10*, 223-229.

O'Sullivan, L.F., Meyer-Bahlburg, H.F.L., & Wasserman, G.A. 2000. The reactions of inner-city boys and their mothers to research interviews about sex. *Journal of Psychology & Human Sexuality, 12*(1/2).

Paikoff, R.L. (1995). Early heterosexual debut: Situations of sexual possibility during the transition to adolescence. *American Journal of Orthopsychiatry, 65*, 389-401.

Patterson, G.R. (1982). *Coercive family process*. Eugene, OR: Castilia.

Pleak, R.R., & Meyer-Bahlburg, H.F.L. (1990). Sexual behavior and AIDS knowledge in young male prostitutes in Manhattan. *Journal of Sex Research, 27*, 557-587.

Robins, L.N. (1966). *Deviant children grown up: A sociological and psychiatric study of sociopathic personality*. Baltimore: Williams & Wilkins.

Rodgers, J.L., & Rowe, D.C. (1990). Adolescent sexual activity and mildly deviant behavior. *Journal of Family Issues, 11*, 274-293.

Rodgers, J.L., & Rowe, D.C. (1993). Social contagion and adolescent sexual behavior: A developmental EMOSA model. *Psychological Review, 100*, 479-510.

Rosario, M., Meyer-Bahlburg, H.F.L., Hunter, J., Exner, T.M., Gwadz, M., & Keller, A.M. (1996). The psychosexual development of urban lesbian, gay, and bisexual youths. *Journal of Sex Research, 33*, 113-126.

Rotheram-Borus, M.J., Meyer-Bahlburg, H.F.L., Koopman, C., Rosario, M., Exner, T.M., Henderson, R., Matthieu, M., & Gruen, R.S. (1992a). Lifetime sexual behaviors among runaway males and females. *Journal of Sex Research, 29*, 15-29.

Rotheram-Borus, M.J., Meyer-Bahlburg, H.F.L., Rosario, M., Koopman, C., Haignere, C.S., Exner, T.M., Matthieu, M., Henderson, R., & Gruen, R.S. (1992b). Lifetime sexual behaviors among predominantly minority male runaways and gay/bisexual adolescents in New York City. *AIDS Education and Prevention, Supplement,* 34-42, Fall 1992.

Rutter, M., Harrington, R., Quinton, D., and Pickles, A. (1994). Adult outcome of conduct disorder in childhood: Implications for concepts and definitions of patterns of psychopathology. In R.D. Ketterlinus, & M.E. Lamb, *Adolescent problem behaviors. Issues and research* (pp. 57-80). Hillsdale, NJ: Lawrence Erlbaum Associates Publishers.

Sandberg, D.E., Meyer-Bahlburg, H.F.L., Ehrhardt, A.A., & Yager, T.J. (1993). The prevalence of gender-atypical behavior in elementary school children. *Journal of the American Academy of Child and Adolescent Psychiatry, 32,* 306-314.

Sandberg, D.E., Meyer-Bahlburg, H.F.L., & Yager, T.J. (1991). The child behavior checklist nonclinical standardization samples: Should they be utilized as norms? *Journal of the American Academy of Child and Adolescent Psychiatry, 30,* 124-134.

Snook, S.C., & Gorsuch, R.L. (1989). Component analysis versus common factor analysis: A Monte Carlo study. *Psychological Bulletin, 106,* 148-154.

Snyder, J.J., & Patterson, G.R. (1995). Individual differences in social aggression: A test of a reinforcement model of socialization in the natural environment. *Behavior Therapy, 26,* 371-391.

Stanton, B., Li, X., Black, M., Ricardo, I., Galbraith, J., Kaljee, L., & Feigelman, S. (1994). Sexual practices and intentions among preadolescent and early adolescent low-income African-Americans. *Pediatrics, 93,* 966-973.

Udry, J.R. (1994). Integrating biological and sociological models of adolescent problem behaviors. In R.D. Ketterlinus, & M.E. Lamb (Eds.), *Adolescent problem behaviors. Issues and research* (pp. 93-107). Hillsdale, NJ: Lawrence Erlbaum Associates, Publishers.

Zelnik, M., & Shah, F.K. (1983). First intercourse among young Americans. *Family Planning Perspectives, 15,* 64-70.

Zucker, K.J., & Bradley, S.J. (1995). *Gender identity disorder and psychosexual problems in children and adolescents.* New York: The Guilford Press.

Reactions of Inner-City Boys
and Their Mothers
to Research Interviews About Sex

Lucia F. O'Sullivan, PhD
Heino F. L. Meyer-Bahlburg, Dr. rer. nat.
Gail Wasserman, PhD

ABSTRACT. Our understanding of child sexuality is very unsatisfactory, in part because research in this area has progressed slowly due to concerns of parents, institutional review boards, school authorities, granting and community agents. Some members of these groups worry that this line of inquiry will have adverse consequences, such as causing

Lucia F. O'Sullivan, Heino F. L. Meyer-Bahlburg, and Gail Wasserman are affiliated with New York State Psychiatric Institute and College of Physicians and Surgeons of Columbia University, New York, NY.

Address correspondence to Heino F. L. Meyer-Bahlburg, Dr. rer. nat., NYSPI Unit 10, 722 West 168th Street, New York, NY 10032; email address: (meyerb@child.cpmc.columbia.edu).

The authors thank the mothers and sons for their participation, and Dinah Gay, Richard Austin, Yvette Bueno, Sherill Campbell, and Maryam Muhammad for their help with data collection and coding.

This research was supported in part by NIMH Center Grant 2-P50-MH43520 to Anke A. Ehrhardt, a NIMH Fellowship Training Grant T32-MH19139 to Lucia F. O'Sullivan, a Sexuality Research Fellowship from the Social Science Research Council to Lucia F. O'Sullivan, and a grant from the Leon Lowenstein Foundation to Gail Wasserman.

A preliminary report of the data was presented as a poster at the 22nd Annual Meeting of the International Academy of Sex Research, Rotterdam, Netherlands, June 26-30, 1996.

[Haworth co-indexing entry note]: "Reactions of Inner-City Boys and Their Mothers to Research Interviews About Sex." O'Sullivan, Lucia F., Heino F. L. Meyer-Bahlburg, and Gail Wasserman. Co-published simultaneously in *Journal of Psychology & Human Sexuality* (The Haworth Press, Inc.) Vol. 12, No. 1/2, 2000, pp. 81-103; and: *Childhood Sexuality: Normal Sexual Behavior and Development* (ed: Theo G. M. Sandfort, and Jany Rademakers) The Haworth Press, Inc., 2000, pp. 81-103. Single or multiple copies of this article are available for a fee from The Haworth Document Delivery Service [1-800-342-9678, 9:00 a.m. - 5:00 p.m. (EST). E-mail address: getinfo@haworthpressinc.com].

distress in child participants or stimulating them to engage in sexual activities. The current study constitutes an exploratory investigation of the reactions of 98 boys (7-13 years) and their 84 mothers after completing individual interviews as part of a larger HIV-related study on the development of sexual behaviors. Most boys reported feeling positively about their participation, were not upset by any aspects of their participation, and indicated willingness to participate again. Most mothers had similar positive reactions. However, considerable reticence was noted on behalf of some boys in their responses to sexual knowledge questions as compared to other portions of the interview. This reticence appeared attributable primarily to limited sexual vocabulary knowledge, and learned inhibitions regarding sex talk with adults. Further refinement of methodologies appropriate for interviewing children about sex is needed. *[Article copies available for a fee from The Haworth Document Delivery Service: 1-800-342-9678. E-mail address: <getinfo@ haworthpressinc.com> Website: <http://www.HaworthPress.com>]*

KEYWORDS. Research methods, sex interviews, child assessment

Our understanding of the development of sexual behavior has typically been derived from descriptive studies employing retrospective reports from adolescent and adult samples (e.g., Kinsey, Pomeroy, & Martin, 1948; Kinsey, Pomeroy, Martin, & Gebhard, 1953; Rotheram-Borus et al., 1992a, 1992b), and surveys using parents' reports of their children's sexual behavior (e.g., Achenbach, 1991; Friedrich, Grambsch, Broughton, Kuiper, & Beilke, 1991). Other information about childhood sexual behavior comes from studies of pubertal development (e.g., Udry, 1994), child sexual abuse (e.g., Cosentino, Meyer-Bahlburg, Alpert, Weinberg, & Gaines, 1995), or the development of "problem behaviors" (e.g., Jessor & Jessor, 1977).

Rarely have researchers studied the development of sexual behavior by means of direct inquiry of children themselves, with some exceptions (e.g., Broderick, 1966, Elias & Gebhard, 1969; Paikoff, 1995; Stanton et al., 1994). Objections of some parents, individual members of institutional review boards, school authorities, granting and community agents have effectively discouraged or prevented many researchers from interviewing children directly about their sexual behavior (Goldman, 1994). These groups are concerned that involving children in studies of sexual behavior may have adverse consequences, such as causing distress in children or prompting sexual experimentation.

In essence, the study of child sexuality challenges a cherished belief in children's fundamental asexuality and "innocence" (Craft, 1994; Jackson, 1990). According to Goldman (1994, p. 6) "Childhood itself is subject to even more social taboos where sexuality is concerned than is adolescence." She believes that "strong taboos still operate to limit enquiry, public and private, by protest, political and institutional obstruction, and the exercise of moral censorship," particularly in the realm of child sexuality. These "sexual taboos" serve to deny recognition of sexuality in children and young adolescents and protect youth from the "contamination" of sexual information. In line with this thinking, some school authorities and parents argue that talking to children about sex may distress younger children, "put ideas into innocent heads," and prompt or condone sexual behavior in adolescents (Lenderyou, 1994; Thomson, 1994). School authorities restrict access to children for research and educational purposes to accommodate those parents who feel that discussions with children about sex are inappropriate (Kirby, 1992). In their cross-national study of children's sexual cognition, Goldman and Goldman (1982) experienced the most problems conducting their research in the United States, especially with regard to convincing school administrators and principals to provide access to schools, obtaining consent from parents, and gaining approval of their research measures.

However, studies of child sexuality are typically held up much earlier than the data collection phase of the research process. Problems frequently arise in the proposal stage. Institutional review boards (IRB) tend to view surveys about personal matters, such as sexuality, to be "exceptionally stressful or anxiety-producing" for participants (Nolan, 1992, p. 9). For example, in a survey of 78 chairs of institutional review boards regarding the most important topics requiring IRB attention, the chairs listed (in order) research on illegal activities, research involving children, "socially sensitive research" which refers to research with notable political and moral implications, and AIDS (Sieber & Baluyot, 1992). Given these views, research proposals involving interviews with children about sex clearly attract significant IRB attention and concern. In cases where an alternative design can not be employed, such proposals are likely to be rejected by IRBs and, thus, unlikely to be submitted for funding. In fact, research proposals involving socially sensitive topics such as child sexuality are twice as likely to be rejected by institutional review boards compared to research proposals involving less sensitive topics (Ceci, Peters, & Plotkin, 1985). Frayser (1993) has noted that what is known about child sexuality is typically produced in the context of investigations of "legitimate" topics of study, such as gender identity and sexual abuse, as a consequence of objections raised about more direct inquiries.

Due to the paucity of research on surveying children about sex, it is difficult to counter concerns about the well-being of child participants. There is substantial evidence that *educating* children about sexuality matters does not produce adverse consequences, such as prompting early onset of sexual behavior (see Visser & van Bilsen, 1994, for a review). However, it is not clear whether children would be distressed by direct inquiry regarding sexual matters. Therefore, the purpose of the current study is to explore the nature of boys' and their mothers' immediate reactions to interviews about sex. Although the current study was designed to investigate the development of sexual problem behaviors rather than specifically the reactions to interviews about sex, per se, informal observations during the interview evaluations as well as assessments conducted after completion of the comprehensive interview protocol captured boys' and mothers' personal evaluations and feelings about various aspects of their participation, including aspects of the study that they liked and disliked, questions that caused them worry, and willingness to participate again if asked to do so.

In addition, we wanted to determine whether it was possible to differentiate boys who reported being unwilling to participate again from those who reported willingness. A child's reported willingness or unwillingness to participate again may be a useful index of his or her overall reaction to the interviewing experience. We expected that willingness to participate again may be related to duration of the interview. Longer duration of participation may be associated with poorer ability to attend and maintain interest in the interview, and thus unwillingness to participate again. Longer duration may also be associated with greater inhibitions regarding discussions with adults about sexual issues. Second, we expected that children who reported feeling worried about themselves as a result of their participation may be more likely to report unwillingness compared to those boys who did not report concerns. Finally, we hypothesized that unwilling boys would be younger and have more adjustment problems compared to their counterparts. These boys may be less attentive, more easily bored, and/or less willing to comply with interviewers' requests.

METHOD

Participants

Participants were 98 boys and their 84 mothers recruited to participate in a study of the development of sexual problem behaviors from a longitudinal study of the development of disruptive behavior in a high-risk sample of boys. The methodology of the longitudinal study has been described elsewhere in detail (Wasserman, Miller, Pinner, & Jaramillo, 1996). The boys were brothers of juvenile offenders seen in the New York Family Court system and, at the time of the assessment on which this report is based, ranged in age from 7.0 years to 13.8 years (M = 10.4 years). Most of the boys were fairly evenly split between the third (21.4%), fourth (20.4%) and fifth (23.5%) grades. Only one boy was not attending school at the time of the study. Most of the families were African-American (54.5%) or Hispanic (42.4%). Few participants were from other ethnic groups (3.0%). The highest level of schooling completed by mothers was on average the eleventh grade. Mothers' occupational status received an average rating of 23.4 (range 13.00-54.12) (Stevens & Cho, 1985) which is comparable to the income of a child healthcare worker.

MEASURES

AIDS and Sexuality Protocol

As part of the larger study of the development of sexual problem behaviors, a battery of questionnaires was orally administered to participants after completing the consent procedure. These questionnaires were followed by a Reaction to Study interview. The entire protocol was approved by the Columbia University Department of Psychiatry Institutional Review Board.

Boys' protocol. Eight instruments were included in the boy's battery including a child's version of a questionnaire assessing the child's gender role behavior and a comprehensive questionnaire assessing the child's social network. These were followed by questions about the child's heterosocial experiences (partly selected from Broderick, 1965) which included items that assessed whether the boy had a girl-friend at that time or ever, how old he was when he first had a girl-friend (if applicable), whether he had ever participated in kissing games, whether he had "seriously" kissed a girl, how old he was when he first "seriously" kissed a girl (if applicable), and what he meant when he referred to a serious (special) kiss. Boys were then administered a questionnaire assessing loneliness followed by an interview designed to assess the boy's knowledge about some basic sexual matters (Sexual Knowledge, using three questions from Goldman & Goldman, 1982, pp. 192 and 217). The three open-ended questions were: (1) "How can anyone know that a newborn baby is a boy or a girl?" (2) "Do the bodies of boys and girls grow differently as they grow older?" and (3) "How are babies made?" Each question could be followed by probes. The sexual knowledge portion of the child's protocol was followed by three measures of the child's AIDS knowledge and attitudes, designed for this study, to assess comfort with and acquaintance of a person with AIDS, as well as perceived vulnerability to AIDS infection. The average approximate duration of the boys' protocols (including some brief breaks for most) was 2.0 hours (range 55 minutes to 3 hours and 50 minutes).

Mothers' protocol. Sixteen questionnaires were orally administered to mothers in the following order: a measure of their sons' social network; two questionnaires of their son's gender role behavior in the past six months followed by the life versions of these two measures; two measures assessing knowledge and attitudes about tuberculosis; three measures of knowledge and attitudes about AIDS or STDS; two measures of the child's sexual behavior in the past six months; a guilt inventory; a lifetime measure of the child's sexual behavior; a measure of the child's sexual socialization; and a religious practices question-naire. The average approximate duration of the mother's protocol was 3.1 hours (range 2 hours 6 minutes to 4 hours and 55 minutes).

Reaction to Study Questionnaires

The protocols of both boys and mothers ended with a Reaction-to-Study questionnaire.

Boys' version. This orally administered questionnaire consisted of 11 questions designed to assess boys' reactions upon completion of the entire interview protocol (including the sex portions of the interview). These questions included feelings about participating in the study, whether there was anything about the study that they did not like or that bothered them a lot, whether there was anything about the study that they liked a lot, which (if any) of the questions made them worry about themselves, feelings about participating again if asked to do so, and reasons for their unwillingness, if applicable. Boys were also asked if they were upset by questions related to their friends, AIDS, girlfriends, reproduction, and differences between boys and girls.

Mothers' version. The mothers' version consisted of 13 self-report, open-ended questions parallel in form to the items in the boys' version. In addition, mothers were asked which of the questions (if any) made them worry about their son, the ways in which they believed the study could help others, if at all, and the ways in which they believed the study could harm others, if at all. Using a close-ended format similar to the boys' version, mothers reported whether they were upset by questions related to AIDS, their son's sexual behavior, their own sexuality, and their child-rearing practices.

Data from the Disruptive Behavior Study

Mothers completed the Child Behavior Checklist (CBCL; Achenbach, 1991) during their earlier participation in the disruptive behavior study. Each boy's CBCL Total score was used in the current study as an index of the extent to which he exhibited problem behaviors.

Interviewer Ratings

After each session, interviewers rated the participant's cooperation on a 4-point scale ranging from *poor* (1) to *very good* (4) to provide additional information regarding the participants' reactions and overall reliability of the interview. They also rated the quality of the interview overall and the quality of sections of the protocol on a 4-point scale ranging from *unsatisfactory* (1) to *high quality* (4). For low quality ratings (i.e., "1" or "2"), interviewers indicated the likely reason(s) on a checklist of 13 possible reasons (e.g., participant was bored or uninterested, did not want to be more specific, was uncomfortable with the topic).

Procedure

Mothers were approached after completing their participation with their sons in the second-year wave of the ongoing disruptive-behavior study. They were asked to participate in the AIDS and Sexuality protocol and informed that they would be compensated financially for their participation and for any travel expenses incurred. All but one of the 98 mothers who were approached agreed to participate. Of these, 99 boys and their 86 mothers were interviewed individually, most within 3.7 months of the first approach (range 0 to 10 months). One boy and two mothers did not complete the Reaction to Study questionnaire. As to the remaining mothers who originally agreed to participate, their whereabouts could not be determined ($n = 3$), or else they later refused to participate ($n = 5$), had moved away ($n = 2$), or the family had separated ($n = 1$). Thus, the final sample consisted of 98 boys and their 84 mothers.

Sixty-eight families were interviewed in our offices at Columbia-Presbyterian Medical Center, and the remaining 18 families were interviewed in their homes. Prior to conducting the interviews, mothers were given a copy of the consent form to follow as the interviewer read through it or to read for themselves. They were asked to provide consent for their own and each son's participation. Eleven mothers had two sons who participated in the study and one mother had three sons; all others provided consent for one son. Boys were asked to read and sign a child assent form and assistance was given as needed. Families were given copies of these forms to keep. Any questions about the study were addressed by the interviewer. The interviews were conducted in English for all boys and 63 mothers, and in Spanish for the remaining 23 mothers. Participants completed the AIDS and Sexuality protocol followed by the Reaction to Study questionnaire. Interviews were audiotaped for all participants except those for six families who did not provide consent to do so. The boys were rewarded with snacks and access to blocks, puzzles, board or computer games after completing sections of the protocol to counteract inattention and boredom resulting from the lengthy interview.

The boys and mothers were interviewed individually by a trained interviewer. Of five interviewers, one was an African-American man, three were African-American women, and one was a Hispanic woman. Four interviewers were in their early 20s, and one female interviewer was in her mid-30s.

Data Preparation

Ninety-eight boys and 84 mothers completed the Reaction to Study questionnaire after the AIDS and Sexuality protocol. Two study coordinators reviewed all open-ended responses provided in the Reaction to Study to develop coding categories. Two raters were then trained to code the open-ended responses of the Parent version and Child version separately using 10 randomly selected questionnaires from each version. Both raters independently rated all remaining questionnaires. The interrater reliability for the remaining questionnaires was excellent: the median Kappa score for the Parent version was .95 (range .58 to 1.00) and the median Kappa score for the child version was .96 (range 0.72 to 1.00).

RESULTS

Characteristics of the Interview Process

The boys' interviews about sexual knowledge were unexpectedly long; the median duration was approximately 24.0 minutes (range 5.0 to 74.0 minutes, the latter including a break). In contrast to other parts of the protocol, many boys became markedly slower in responding, there were long silences, and the boys' behavior, mimics, and affect changed from ready cooperation to reticence.

A number of interviewing techniques (Meyer-Bahlburg, 1995) were used to overcome the apparent inhibitions experienced by some boys in responding to the sexual knowledge portions of the interview. One technique involved stressing to the child that the interview was a "special" environment in which he was allowed to say anything he liked without repercussion, noting that nothing he said would be reported to his mother, and describing the difficulties about speaking aloud that were overcome by other boys who had participated earlier in the study. Other techniques used to promote cooperation included instructing the child to write or draw the word instead of saying it aloud, to spell the word instead of saying it, or whispering the word into the tape-recorder while the interviewer was outside of the room.

The following transcript illustrates one 12-year old boy's difficulties. Prior to this interaction, the interviewer had reminded the boy that his answers would be confidential, he was allowed to use any words that he wanted, and his answers would be confidential.

(I)nterviewer: How can anyone know that a newborn baby is a boy or a girl? After an 8-second pause, the interviewer repeated the question. *(P)articipant:* By the stomach.

> *I:* Uh-huh?
> *P:* And by the . . . by the . . . by the . . . the doctor puts that thing on her stomach. I seen it on T.V.
> *I:* Uh-huh.
> *P:* I seen it on T.V. That's it.
> *I:* What do they see on T.V.? (8 second pause)
> *P:* They see the . . . the private.
> *I:* Uh-huh. And what do you call the private?
> *P:* Like . . . like "dick" or "pussy."
> *I:* Okay . . . Who has the dick and who has the pussy?
> *P:* Huh?
> *I:* Who has the dick and who has the pussy?
> *P:* Girl has the pussy and the boy got the dick!
> *I:* Are there any other words that you know for "dick" or "pussy" that a grown-up may use, or your mom may use? Are there any other words that you know?
> *P:* No.
> *I:* Or that you may have heard?
> *P:* Yeah . . . (5 second pause)
> *I:* What are they?
> *P:* Nothing.
> *I:* No other words?
> *P:* Nuh-uh.

Following this interaction, the interviewer described how another 12-year old boy that he interviewed earlier had been embarrassed but was able to say other words that he knew. He asked the boy again if he knew of any other words, but the boy said he did not. When the interviewer thanked the boy for his response to the (first) question and rewarded him with a piece of candy, the boy eagerly asked if the interview was over.

Reported Positive and Negative Aspects of Participation

General reactions to participation. Both boys and mothers were asked to report their feelings about participating in the study. The majority of boys (96%) indicated that they felt positively about their participation and 4% reported feeling negatively. Similarly, 92% of the mothers reported feeling positive, 7% felt neutral or unsure, and only one mother (1%) reported negative feelings about participating in the study.

Positive aspects of participation. To determine which aspects of participation were perceived as positive or rewarding, both boys and mothers were asked whether there was anything about the study that they liked a lot. More than three-quarters of the boys (76%) and almost all mothers (93%) responded affirmatively (see Table 1). The boys who responded affirmatively were then asked to specify what they had liked. These boys were most likely to respond in general terms without elaborating further. When they did elaborate, the most frequently reported positive aspect of the study was the rewards provided in the study, such as playing with Lego and eating "treats." A few mentioned increased awareness about AIDS and STDs. For example, one 10-year old boy responded "Yes, talking about AIDS so when I grow up I can use safe sex." A miscellaneous cluster of responses included nonspecific factors associated with their participation, such as interacting with the staff.

The mothers who reported liking something about the study also commonly did not elaborate on the positive aspects of their participation (see Table 1). However, those who did elaborate typically reported increased awareness about AIDS/STDs or TB. Mothers (but not boys) were also asked whether they believed that the study would be of help to others in some way. Almost all mothers ($n = 81$; 96.4%) reported that they believed the study would be of help with reasons corresponding to the aspects of participation that they reported liking. Specifically, participation was perceived as being of help to others because of its potential use as a learning tool (16.7%) or to raise awareness generally (11.9%). One woman said, "Yes. It brings questions to mind that if you're an ordinary mother you wouldn't think of these things." Another mother said, "Parents will keep their eyes more open. Little questions were asked to help parents be more aware." Another said, "Yes, the questions helped, helped me realize

TABLE 1. Boys' and Mothers' Reports of Anything About the Study that They Liked a Lot[a]

	Boys	Mothers
Characteristic	(%)	(%)
All of it (no elaboration)	14.3	8.3
Some of it (no elaboration)	27.6	15.5
Increased awareness generally	0.0	15.5
Increased awareness about AIDS/STDs	7.1	20.2
Increased awareness about TB	0.0	19.0
Increased awareness about sex and reproduction	2.0	0.0
Something relevant to child or children	—[b]	16.7
Rewards in study	14.3	1.2
Other	10.2	16.7

Note. N = 98 boys and N = 84 mothers.
[a] Some subjects endorsed more than one response.
[b] This category was not used to code responses.

that I need to sit down with my children and tell them straight out and can't hold anything back." Others believed that the study would help mothers learn more about their child's behavior (7.1%) or about AIDS, STDs, and TB (13.1%).

Negative aspects of participation. When asked whether there was anything about the study that they did not like or that bothered them a lot, one-quarter of the boys (26%) and one-fifth of the mothers (18%) responded affirmatively (see Table 2). When asked to elaborate, the 25 boys described feeling uncomfortable answering sex questions, having to use words that they perceived as being "bad," or lacking answers for the interviewers' questions. One 8-year old boy told the interviewer that he was bothered by "Talking about the private spots . . . Because no one ever asked me a question about that before." With reference to the open-ended question about physical differences between men and women, one 10-year old boy who had difficulty generating answers to these questions said he was bothered by "the test when a woman doesn't have any clothes on and a man doesn't have any clothes on. It was hard." Another 8-year old boy who had difficulty answering the sex knowledge questions said that he was bothered by questions "about where babies come from. . . . That I didn't know what it is." Responding to the length of the study, one 11-year old boy complained to his interviewer, "You talk too much. Read too much."

Overall, seventeen children (17.4%) reported not liking a sex-related aspect of the interview.

Of the 15 mothers who reported disliking or being bothered by something about the study, reasons relating to the interview duration or the sexually explicit nature of the questions were reported most frequently. Six mothers (7.1%) reported not liking at least one sex-related aspect of the interview. One woman said, "Some questions were explicit or a little strong. For example, Did your son put something in his anus? This type of question bothers me." Another woman responded, "[It] makes you feel strange that children had to think about sex in such a way," and another said, "[I] just don't like answering a whole bunch of private questions, but okay."

Reported Worry Resulting from Participation

To assess further the extent to which subjects perceived negative effects of their participation in the study, both boys and mothers were asked whether any of the interview questions made them worry about themselves or worry that there might be something wrong that they had not thought of before. Eighteen boys reported such worry. The focus of concern was typically the HIV/AIDS questions (with no further elaboration provided) ($n = 11$). The specific HIV/AIDS transmission questions and sex-related questions were reported less frequently ($n = 3$ in both cases), and the other responses could not be coded ($n = 2$). For example, one 10-year old boy responded "I'm

TABLE 2. Boys' and Mothers' Reports of Anything About the Study that They Did Not Like or that Bothered Them a Lot[a]

Characteristic	Boys (%)	Mothers (%)
Uncomfortable answering sex questions	14.3	2.4
Explicit nature of questions for parent	—[b]	3.6
Explicit nature of questions for son	—[b]	2.4
Use of "bad" words	3.1	—[b]
Lack of knowledge	3.1	1.2
AIDS questions increased anxiety	2.0	2.4
Interview duration	1.0	3.6
Other	4.1	2.4

Note. $N = 98$ boys and $N = 84$ mothers.
[a] Some subjects endorsed more than one response.
[b] This category was not used to code responses.

scared I might catch AIDS." Following this open-ended question, the interviewer also directly inquired about whether each of five particular types of questions had upset them. Of the 98 boys interviewed, 4.1% reported being upset by questions about their friends, 13.3% by questions about AIDS, 9.2% by questions about girlfriends, 17.3% by questions about where babies come from, and 10.2% by questions about how boys and girls are different. Thus, a minority of boys reported being upset by each of the five types of questions.

Fifteen mothers reported worrying about themselves as a result of their participation. Of these mothers, the most frequently reported questions related to TB transmission ($n = 4$). The other issues included questions about sex ($n = 2$), HIV/AIDS (not elaborated) ($n = 2$), HIV/AIDS transmission ($n = 1$), parental responsibilities ($n = 2$), and "others" ($n = 4$).

Using another open-ended question, mothers were asked whether any questions had made them worry about their sons. Ten mothers (11.9%) reported that they had such concerns. Specifically, the concerns of these ten mothers related to questions concerning sexual behavior ($n = 3$), HIV/AIDS ($n = 2$) their son's social network ($n = 2$), child sexual abuse ($n = 2$), or their son's behavior ($n = 1$). Mothers were also asked directly whether they were upset by each of four particular question categories used in the study. Seven mothers (8.3%) reported being upset by the AIDS questions; six (7.1%) by questions related to their son's sexual behavior, three (3.6%) by questions related to their own sexual behavior, and one (1.2%) by the child-rearing questions. All other mothers reported that they had not been upset by these categories of questions.

To gain additional information about concerns resulting from participation in the interview, mothers (but not boys) were also asked whether they believed that the study may be of harm to others. Four mothers (4.8%) indicated that they believed that it might, and three of these mothers elaborated on their response. One mother thought parents may possibly react badly to their participation if they were trying to conceal information from the interviewer. Another explained that parents may think that their child is gay as a result of completing the interview which might cause distress in the parents about this typically undesired possibility, and the last reported that a participant might worry later about issues that arose in the interview if they had lied during the interview. Another mother qualified her answer with "No, but some questions may be offensive to some people." An additional two mothers were unsure about whether the study may be of harm to others.

Willingness to Participate Again

Both boys and mothers described how they would feel about participating in "something like this again" if someone asked them to do so. The majority of both the boys (79.6%) and the mothers (91.7%) reported that they would be willing. Of the remaining boys, 13 (13.3%) reported that they would be unwilling and 7 (7.1%) reported that they would be unsure about their willingness to participate again. Of the remaining mothers, four (4.8%) indicated that they would be unwilling to participate again and three (3.6%) indicated uncertainty about their willingness. The four unwilling mothers and the 13 unwilling boys were not from the same families. However, two of the three mothers who were unsure about their willingness to participate again were parents of two of the seven unsure boys.

Reasons for unwillingness. Of the 13 boys who reported that they would not want to participate again, four would not elaborate on their response. For those boys who did elaborate, their unwillingness typically related to the length of the study ($n = 3$), difficulty with the questions ($n = 2$), or discomfort discussing sex ($n = 1$). Boys reported unwillingness "because it's tiring," "because it takes too long," and "because I got everything out of my system and talked about everything here." Examples of other responses were "It's too hard," and "because I hate when they asked me a lot of questions and when they ask me questions about girls and babies." In three cases, the boys' responses were not audiotaped or recorded. The boys who reported being unsure about their unwillingness unfortunately did not elaborate and/or were not prompted to elaborate by the interviewer. Of the four unwilling mothers, two cited that the length of the study was prohibitive, one indicated that the nature of the questions was discomforting, and one mother's response was not recorded by the interviewer. For the three mothers who were unsure of their willingness to participate again, two would not elaborate and the response of the third mother was not recorded.

Predicting Unwillingness in Boys

A number of variables were examined to determine their usefulness in distinguishing those boys who reported being unwilling to participate again in a similar study from those who reported being willing. These variables included length of time to complete the interview, concerns related to participation, as well as age and behavior problems.

Duration of child's participation. We examined whether the willing and unwilling boys differed in the overall duration of their study participation and the duration of their participation in the sex interview portion of the survey specifically. (Data for these two durations were available for less than half of the sample of boys due to inconsistencies in interviewers' reporting practices.) The analysis revealed that boys who reported unwillingness to participate again took longer to complete the sex portion of the interview, $F(1, 45) = 8.82$, $p < .01$, but did not take longer to complete the whole interview, $F(1, 43) = 0.01$, $p > .05$, compared to boys who reported willingness to participate again.

Worry resulting from participation. A higher proportion of boys who reported worrying as a result of participating in the study to subsequently reported being unwilling to participate again compared to those boys who did not report worry, $X^2(1) = 4.56$, $p < .05$.

Background variables. Boys who reported willingness to participate again in a similar future study did not differ significantly from those who reported unwillingness in terms of age, $F(1, 97) = 1.76$, $p > .05$, nor in terms of CBCL Total scores, $F(1, 97) = 0.45$, $p > .05$.

Interviewer Ratings

An additional index of participants' reactions to the sex interviews was provided by interviewers' quality ratings of subject participation. The majority of boys' (91.0%) and mothers' (94.9%) interviews received a reliability rating of *high quality* or *generally reliable quality* (i.e., a score of 3 or higher on a 4-point scale). Eight interviews with boys were rated as having questionable ($n = 7$) or unsatisfactory ($n = 1$) overall quality. The reasons checked by the interviewers for the eight low reliability ratings for boys were that the boys did not feel comfortable with the topic ($n = 7$), did not understand or speak English well ($n = 6$), and/or were bored or uninterested ($n = 5$). (More than one reason could be provided). The boy who received the unsatisfactory rating reported negative feelings about his participation; the other seven boys reported positive feelings. None of these boys reported being bothered by aspects of the study, all but one reported liking aspects of the study, and all but two reported concerns as a result of participating in the study. In addition, all but two of these boys reported being willing to participate again (one boy indicated he was unsure about his willingness and one reported being unwilling).

The reasons for the five low ratings for mothers typically related to being bored or disinterested ($n = 3$), not wanting to be more specific ($n = 2$), seeming emotionally unstable ($n = 2$), having trouble remembering ($n = 2$), thinking the interview took too long ($n = 2$), and/or refusing to give information for various section of the interview ($n = 2$).

Interviewers rated the cooperation of most boys (94.9%) and mothers (94.9%) as *good* or *very good* (i.e., a score of 3 or higher on a 4-point scale) for the whole protocol. All but one of the boys who participated in this study was rated as being at least fairly cooperative (i.e., a score of "2" or higher on a 4-point scale). For the uncooperative boy, the quality ratings for each of the sections of his interview was rated as unsatisfactory as was the overall rating of the quality of the interview. The interviewer described the 9-year old boy as being bored, depressed, emotionally unstable, and withholding of information. Although this boy reported being unsure whether he would participate again in the future if asked to do so, he also reported feeling positive about his participation, said he was not bothered or concerned by any aspects of the study, and liked the rewards he had earned.

DISCUSSION

The Reaction-to-Study interview is a routine procedure specifically tailored to each research protocol. It is used at the end of all of our projects to examine a participant's reactions and provide debriefing, on-the-spot counseling, if indicated, or referral to mental-health services on the rare occasion. It was the unexpectedly long duration of the sex knowledge portion of the sexual problem behavior study and the difficulties many boys demonstrated in answering its questions that compelled us to analyze the Reaction-to-Study for the sample as a whole, as well as our recurrent encounters with the concerns of institutional review boards and other agencies about sexual interviewing.

Therefore, this study constitutes a pilot or exploratory examination of children's and mothers' reactions to inquiry about sexual matters.

Although the sexual knowledge questions were imbedded in a protocol addressing other topics, some of which were not related to sexual matters, it was clear that the sex-related questions were particularly salient to the boys. Many boys showed obvious reticence when completing the section on sexual knowledge. Interestingly, comparable reactions were not noticed in the section on heterosocial experiences (which, however, did not touch upon specific sexual behaviors, beyond kissing, nor sexual anatomy). In discussing the apparent reticence during the sex knowledge section with the interviewers and reviewing the corresponding audiotapes, we got the impression that there were several factors at play. Most boys knew considerably more, especially about physical sex differences, than they were initially willing to disclose. One of the reasons for their reluctance seemed to be the lack of a vocabulary for the sexual anatomy that they thought acceptable for adults'–especially women's–ears. Although the boys had participated in earlier phases of the longitudinal project, neither of these preceding sessions dealt with sexual matters so presumably for most of these boys participating in a sex interview was a novel experience. With some prodding, however, most of the boys were able to come up with terms. These terms were those used typically by younger children (e.g., "pee-pee" for penis) or as slang (e.g., "dick" for penis). In addition, many boys simply did not know much about the detail of "where babies come from."

More striking to us than the limits in vocabulary and knowledge was the obvious inhibitions many boys showed in responding to our questions, as if they had been asked to do something forbidden. Indeed, boys who reported being unwilling to participate again generally had taken longer to complete the sex-knowledge portion of the protocol than those who reported being willing, although no differences were noted in the times taken to complete the whole interview. Most boys had some knowledge and vocabulary about sexual matters, even though many were obviously not used to talking about such matters with adults in a tolerant setting. In fact, one of the techniques that sometimes helped to facilitate disclosure was having the mother give explicit permission to the boy to talk to us about sexual issues. In preceding qualitative focus group interviews with other mothers from the same ethnic and socioeconomic background, we learned that many of them never had any formal sex education and, indeed, some of these mothers requested our help with educating their children about sex. Moreover, some mothers gave dramatic examples of very punitive reactions of their own parents when sexual issues came up or examples of the extent to which they had avoided talking to others about sexual matters. For instance, one woman who had not been prepared for menarche by anyone was deeply troubled by its occurrence, but took half a year to gather the courage to let someone, her older sister, know of her secret in order to find out what it might be.

Similarly, the boys in the current study who had difficulties in talking about sexual matters seemed to have internalized parental prohibitions about sex talk. These prohibitions may have delayed their acquisition of an appropriate vocabulary and set up a conditioned inhibition of conversations about sexual matters with adults. The assumed internalization of negative reactions by the parents is also compatible with the labeling of sex topics and sex words as "nasty" by some of the boys. The reticence noted in this sample of boys when asked questions about sex may be attributable, in part, to characteristics of the sample itself. These boys lived in economically depressed inner-city areas of New York and came from families with generally low educational and economic attainment. Moreover, they would not have received formal sex education in their schools until they were older.

Children's experience of parental disapproval with regard to communication about sex in Western culture and particularly the United States is well known (e.g., Gagnon & Simon, 1973; Gadpaille, 1975; Goldman & Goldman, 1982, pp. 304-306). However, we found it to be stronger in our sample than we expected based on the senior author's (HMB) experience in a clinic setting with children and adolescents from similar demographic backgrounds. Once we realized the difficulties experienced by our sample, we trained the interviewers in the use of several techniques applied successfully in the clinic setting to facilitate disclosure by reticent children (Meyer-Bahlburg, 1995). As a consequence, the average time needed for completion of the sex-knowledge section seemed to decrease considerably although, unfortunately, we did not document this systematically. The very fact that we had to introduce these techniques reflects inhibitions of verbalization on the boys' part, and even when these techniques were employed indices of inhibition in the boys' mimics and behavior remained. It is clear from our experience that interviewers for research interviews with children about sexuality require special training that goes beyond that needed for sexuality interviews of adolescents and adults (Gruen & Meyer-Bahlburg, 1992) and needs to take into account the apparent inhibitions and vocabulary deficiencies noted in this study.

It should be noted, however, that almost all boys and mothers reported feeling positively about their participation in the study despite some discomfort in talking about sexual matters. As to specific aspects they liked a lot, boys frequently cited rewards that they received for participation which probably reflects, in part, the age of the children as well as their disadvantaged socioeconomic backgrounds. Mothers frequently cited increased awareness and learning. Those boys and mothers who reported disliking something about the study tended to cite reasons related to discomfort with sex questions and the long duration of the study. Surprisingly, apparent inhibitions on behalf of the boys and their inability to maintain attention throughout the interview (according to the interviewers' reports) was not necessarily related to negative interviewing experiences (according to participants' reports).

Perhaps the most important index of participants' reactions to interviews about sex is their willingness to participate again. The majority of both boys and their mothers reported being willing which supports the finding of positive reactions to the study overall. Of the unwilling participants, only one boy and one mother attributed their reluctance explicitly to the sexual aspects of the interview. The others were more likely to attribute reluctance to the duration of the study or else did not elaborate. The generally high level of willingness is particularly gratifying given the nature of the sample, brothers of adjudicated delinquents, a sample that may be expected to be more oppositional than other samples of similarly aged boys.

Although many boys gave some indications of discomfort and needed some help in communicating with the interviewers about sexual matters, neither they nor their mothers showed strong adverse emotional reactions. No one needed significant on-the-spot counseling for emotional problems, no interview-related referral to mental-health services was necessary, and none of the mothers contacted us after the study about any untoward reactions of their sons. Even though some boys and mothers commented about their discomfort with or dislike of some of the sexual questions, these reactions did not have a clinically significant degree of severity. Thus, we do not have any reason to assume that the sex-knowledge interview exposes children to significant emotional risk. On the other hand, our experiences illustrate the need for improved child-parent communication about sexual matters, especially given the dearth of formal educational school programs about sexuality, AIDS, and STDs for children of elementary-school age in the U.S.

In future investigations, further development of interviewing techniques to facilitate children's disclosure would prove most advantageous. Use of visual techniques, such as cartoons, film clips, drawings, or puzzles, may help children to become more comfortable with the topic. If adolescent discussion groups are a useful guide, conducting initial interviews with two or more children may diminish children's inhibitions, especially if the group includes a child who can model comfort responding to questions about sex. The utility of interactive computer or video programs for this age group should also be explored.

In summary, this exploratory study of children's and mother's reactions to interviews about sex revealed significant reticence on behalf of some boys in responding to questions about sexual knowledge presumably because of limits in vocabulary and knowledge, and the experience of sex-talk prohibitions. However, participants generally reported positive reactions overall. Indeed, concerns about significant distress on behalf of children who participate in interviews about sex seem unwarranted. These findings offer assurance at a time when information about the sexual behavior of children is notably absent from the literature. We hope our findings will prompt researchers to conduct more systematic analyses of children's reactions to interviews about sex and develop more effective means of interviewing children about sex.

REFERENCES

Achenbach, T.M. (1991). *Manual for the Child Behavior Checklist/4-18 and 1991 Profile*. Burlington, VT: University of Vermont Department of Psychiatry.

Broderick, C.B. (1965). Social heterosexual development among urban negroes and whites. *Journal of Marriage and the Family, 27*, 200-203.

Broderick, C.B. (1966). Socio-sexual development in a suburban community. *The Journal of Sex Research, 2*, 1-24.

Ceci, S.J., Peters, D., & Plotkin, J. (1985). Human subjects review, personal values, and the regulation of social science research. *American Psychologist, 40*, 994-1002.

Consentino, E.C., Meyer-Bahlburg, H.F.L., Alpert, J.L., Weinberg, S.L., & Gaines, R. (1995). Sexual behavior problems and psychopathology symptoms in sexually abused girls. *Journal of the American Academy of Child and Adolescent Psychiatry, 34*, 1033-1042.

Craft, A. (1994). Issues in sex education for people with learning disabilities in the United Kingdom. *Sexual and Marital Therapy, 9*, 145-157.

Elias, J., & Gebhard, P. (1969). Sexuality and sexual learning in childhood. *Phi Delta Kappan, 50*, 401-405.

Frayser, S.G. (1994). Defining normal childhood sexuality: An anthropological approach. *Annual Review of Sex Research, 5*, 173-217.

Friedrich, W.N., Grambsch, P., Broughton, D., Kuiper, J., & Beilke, R.L. (1991). Normative sexual behavior in children. *Pediatrics, 88*, 456-464.

Gadpaille, W.J. (1975). *The cycles of sex.* New York: Charles Scribner's Sons.

Gagnon, J.H., & Simon, W. (1973). *Sexual conduct.* London: Hutchinson.

Goldman, J.D.G. (1994). Some methodological problems in planning, executing and validating a cross-national study of children's sexual cognition. *International Journal of Intercultural Relations, 18*, 1-27.

Goldman, R., & Goldman, J. (1982). *Children's sexual thinking: A comparative study of children aged 5 to 15 years in Australia, North America, Britain, and Sweden.* London: Routledge & Kegan Paul.

Gruen, R.S., & Meyer-Bahlburg, H.F.L. (1992). *Training Manual for Research Interviews about Sexual Behavior.* Unpublished manuscript (available from second author), HIV Center for Clinical and Behavioral Studies, New York State Psychiatric Institute and Department of Psychiatry, Columbia University.

Jackson, S. (1990). Demons and innocents: Western ideas on children's sexuality in historical perspective. In M. Perry (Ed.), *Handbook of sexology: Vol. 7. Childhood and adolescent sexology* (pp. 23-49). Amsterdam: Elsevier.

Jessor, R., & Jessor, S.L. (1977). *Problem behavior and psychological development. A longitudinal study of youth.* New York: Academic Press.

Kinsey, A.C., Pomeroy, W.B., & Martin, C.E. (1948). *Sexual behavior in the human male.* Philadelphia: W.B. Saunders.

Kinsey, A.C., Pomeroy, W.B., Martin, C.E., & Gebhard, P.H. (1953). *Sexual behavior in the human female.* Philadelphia: W.B. Saunders.

Kirby, D. (1992). School-based programmes to reduce sexual risk taking behaviours. *Journal of School Health, 62*, 280-287.

Lenderyou, G. (1994). Sex education: A school-based perspective. *Sexual and Marital Therapy, 9*, 127-144.

Meyer-Bahlburg, H.F.L. (1995). *Guidelines for research interviews with children about sex.* Unpublished manuscript, HIV Center for Clinical and Behavioral Studies, New York State Psychiatric Institute and Department of Psychiatry, Columbia University.

Nolan, K. (1992). Ethical issues: Assent, consent, and behavioral research with adolescents. *AACAP Child and Adolescent Research Notes, 2*, 7-10.

Paikoff, R.L. (1995). Early heterosexual debut: Situations of sexual possibility during the transition to adolescence. *American Journal of Orthopsychiatry, 65*, 389-401.

Rotheram-Borus, M.J., Meyer-Bahlburg, H.F.L., Koopman, C., Rosario, M., Exner, T.M., Henderson, R., Matthieu, M., & Gruen, R.S. (1992a). Lifetime sexual behaviors among runaway males and females. *The Journal of Sex Research, 29*, 15-29.

Rotheram-Borus, M.J., Meyer-Bahlburg, H.F.L., Rosario, M., Koopman, C., Haignere, C.S., Exner, T.M., Matthieu, M., Henderson, R., & Gruen, R. S. (1992b). Lifetime sexual behaviors among predominantly minority male runaways and gay/bisexual adolescents in New York City. *AIDS Education and Prevention, Supplement*, 23-42, Fall 1992.

Sieber, J.E., & Baluyot, R.M. (1992). A survey of IRB concerns about social and behavioral research. *IRB: A Review of Human Subjects Research, 14*(2), 9-10.

Stanton, B., Li, X., Black, M., Ricardo, I., Galbraith, J., Kaljee, L., & Feigelman, S. (1994). Sexual practices and intentions among preadolescent and early adolescent low-income African-Americans. *Pediatrics, 93*, 966-973.

Stevens, G., & Cho, J.H. (1985). Socioeconomic index and the new 1980 census occupational classification scheme. *Social Science Research, 14*, 142-168.

Thomson, R. (1994). Prevention, promotion and adolescent sexuality: The politics of school sex education in England and Wales. *Sexual and Marital Therapy, 9*, 115-126.

Udry, J.R. (1994). Integrating biological and sociological models of adolescent problem behaviors. In R.D. Ketterlinus, & M.E. Lamb (Eds.), *Adolescent problem behaviors: Issues and research* (pp. 93-107). Hillsdale, NJ: Lawrence Erlbaum Associates, Publishers.

Visser, A.P., & van Bilsen, P. (1994). Effectiveness of sex education provided to adolescents. *Patient Education and Counseling, 23*, 147-160.

Wasserman, G.A., Miller, L.S., Pinner, E., & Jaramillo, B. (1996). Parenting predictors of early conduct problems in urban, high-risk boys. *Journal of the American Academy of Child and Adolescent Psychiatry, 35*, 1227-1236.

Sexual Behavior
in Dutch and Belgian Children
as Observed by Their Mothers

Theo G. M. Sandfort, PhD
Peggy T. Cohen-Kettenis, PhD

ABSTRACT. Mothers' observations (N = 670) of child sexual behavior have been collected using an adapted version of the Child Sexual Behavior Inventory as developed by Friedrich et al. (1991). The ages of the boys (N = 351) and girls (N = 319) observed range from 0 to 11 years. The results show that there is a lot of variance in the frequency with which specific sexual behaviors are observed. The occurrence of specific behaviors varies with age. While some behaviors are observed more frequently as the child gets older, others are observed less frequently. Boys and girls only differ in a few behaviors. The finding that the behavioral items form an internally consistent scale suggests that there is a general tendency to show sexually related behaviors, which is more or less strongly present in children, which might be a precursor of differential levels of sexual desires in adults. *[Article copies available for a fee from The Haworth Document Delivery Service: 1-800-342-9678. E-mail address: <getinfo@haworthpressinc.com> Website: <http://www.HaworthPress.com>]*

Theo Sandfort is Researcher, Department of Clinical Psychology, Utrecht University and The Netherlands Institute of Social Sexological Research. Peggy Cohen-Kettenis is Psychologist, Department of Child and Adolescent Psychiatry, Academic Hospital Utrecht.

Address correspondence to Theo G. M. Sandfort, Department of Clinical Psychology, Utrecht University, P.O. Box 80140, 3508 TC Utrecht, Netherlands.

[Haworth co-indexing entry note]: "Sexual Behavior in Dutch and Belgian Children as Observed by Their Mothers." Sandfort, Theo G. M., and Peggy T. Cohen-Kettenis. Co-published simultaneously in *Journal of Psychology & Human Sexuality* (The Haworth Press, Inc.) Vol. 12, No. 1/2, 2000, pp. 105-115; and: *Childhood Sexuality: Normal Sexual Behavior and Development* (ed: Theo G. M. Sandfort, and Jany Rademakers) The Haworth Press, Inc., 2000, pp. 105-115. Single or multiple copies of this article are available for a fee from The Haworth Document Delivery Service [1-800-342-9678, 9:00 a.m. - 5:00 p.m. (EST). E-mail address: getinfo@haworthpressinc.com].

KEYWORDS. Child Sexual Behavior Inventory, parents' observations, age differences, gender differences

INTRODUCTION

A search of the scientific literature on child sexuality shows that a lot of research has been done in the past decades. A closer look at this literature indicates, however, that most of these studies–if not all–focus on child sexual abuse. In the current sexological discourse the child only seems to figure as a subject of abuse. This state of affairs implies that our knowledge of child sexuality is very one-sided. Empirical data about normal sexual development in children are scarce. The focus on abuse and its consequences limits our understanding of the way children sexually develop and the meaning of their experiences for later functioning as sexual partners in intimate relationships.

Research on sexual abuse informs us as to how it might be prevented, how to deal with it and how to respond to its consequences. It remains unclear, though, how one should respond to normal child sexual behavior, as well as what normal child sexuality is. Which consequences do parents' responses to expressions of sexuality in their children have? It is quite likely that the specific attention for sexual abuse, not just in scientific publications but also in society at large, has made parents feel insecure regarding the right way of responding to expressions of child sexuality. At the same time, parents continue to respond to children in ways that will affect their sexuality. In this respect it is quite likely that the child's sexual development will not only be affected by the parents' responses to the child's sexual expressions. Socializing responses of the parent in other areas of development will affect the child's later sexual functioning as well. Which processes are actually at work here remains unclear. Our knowledge in this field remains limited as well. Even though there seems to be a direct practical need, sexual education and its consequences have hardly been studied, either.

The aim of this paper is to explore the occurrence of sexual behavior in children in a wide age range. Which sexual behaviors do children actually perform and how frequently can these behaviors be observed? Is the occurrence of specific behaviors in children related to their gender and age, and to their family background? Is the observation of sexual behavior in children dependent upon characteristics of the observer? In answering these questions we hope to promote a further interest in normal child sexual development.

METHOD

To answer the research questions, a questionnaire was developed, which was included in the editorial pages of the magazine *Ouders van nu (Parents Today)*. This magazine, intended for young parents, averages 180,000 subscriptions per year. The magazine is predominantly distributed in the Netherlands, but also in the Dutch speaking part of Belgium.

The main topics addressed in the questionnaire dealt with sexual behavior in the child and gender role behavior. Additionally, characteristics of the family regarding physical interactions with the children were assessed as well as the level of sexual permissiveness in the mothers. Finally, questions were included regarding characteristics of the mother, the child reported upon, and the family.

To assess parents' observations of child sexual behavior we adapted the Child Sexual Behavior Inventory as developed by Friedrich et al. (1991). Twenty-two items of this list were translated into Dutch. Three behaviors were added which in our opinion are quite ordinary, but were lacking in the original scale. These items are "Plays doctor," "Asks questions about sexuality," and "Draws sexual parts and breasts." The occurrence of these behaviors had to be rated on a four-point scale, ranging from 'never' to 'often.' The items of the behavior scale formed a reliable scale (Chronbach's $\alpha = .78$). Gender role behavior was assessed in the same manner with 4 items (Chronbach's $\alpha = .69$). To avoid global impressions, the parents were asked to report about one specific child in their family. To control for unknown selection effects, we also asked parents to report about their oldest child. Another reason for doing the latter was to promote the inclusion of older children in the sample as much as possible.

Sexual permissiveness of the parent was assessed with 4 items from a sexual attitude scale developed by Van Zessen and Sandfort (1991). The selected items did not refer to child sexuality, but were about sexuality and intimacy among adolescents, homosexuality, masturbation within a steady relationship, and the acceptance of extramarital relationships. Parents had to indicate their (dis)agreement with the various statements on a five-point scale. In this study, the final scale had a somewhat low reliability of .59 (Chronbach's α).

The nature of physical interactions with the child has been assessed by asking the frequency with which the following behaviors occur within the family: "You hug and fondle the child," "Your child sees you in the nude," "You bathe or take a shower together with your child," and "You caress your partner in the presence of your child." These items formed a reliable scale (Chronbach's α = .67). A high score on the scale represents a more affective and open interaction.

The questionnaire has been filled out and returned by 670 women, who were the biological mother of the observed child in most of the cases and the step or adoptive mother in a few other cases. A few questionnaires filled out by fathers (13) and by women who were only caretakers of the children (3) were omitted, to ensure comparability between the responses.

The ages of the women, who filled out the questionnaire ranged from 18 to 45 years; the mean age is 30 years. Most of the women are Dutch (93%); the remaining 7% of the women have the Belgian nationality. Compared to Dutch women in general, the women who filled out the questionnaire have a relatively high level of education. While most families included two children, this number ranged from 1 to 10.

The mothers did not differ regarding background variables in relation to the gender of the child whom they reported about. Women differed in relation to the age of the child they reported about. Older women on average reported about older children (r = .37, p < .001). Furthermore, the older the child, the more likely that it had siblings (r = .50, p < .001). Belgian mothers seemed to be somewhat less sexually permissive than Dutch mothers were (2.51 versus 2.81, t = 3,01, p < .001).

The mothers reported in total about 351 boys and 319 girls (respectively 52% and 48%). The ages of the children ranged from 0 to 11 years. Most children, 72%, were between 2 and 6 years old, while 19% were between 6 and 11 years. The mean age was almost 4 years. The boys and girls reported upon did not differ in age.

The occurrence of the sexual behaviors are reported here as dichotomized scores, indicating whether or not the child had shown the behavior at least a few times. The association between the behaviors and other variables are calculated on the raw scale scores, however.

RESULTS

Table 1 shows that there is a lot of variance in the frequency with which the specific sexual behaviors are observed. Some behaviors, such as touching one's genital parts and touching mother's breasts, are observed in almost all children. Others are rarely observed. Examples of the latter are: imitating sexual behavior with dolls, making sexual sounds, and asking to watch sexually explicit TV. Behaviors such as showing one's sexual parts to adults or to other children were observed in about one out of four children.

Some of the sexual behaviors are more frequently observed in older children, while other behaviors seem to occur less when the child gets

TABLE 1. Observed Sexual Behaviors in Children (0-11 years; percentage endorsement)

Item (abbreviated)	Total[1]	Boys	Girls	r age
Touches own sexual parts	97***	98	96	-.06
Touches breasts	77	74	79	-.16***
Interested in opposite sex	65	65	66	.12**
Plays doctor[2]	60***	55	65	.21***
Asks questions about sexuality[2]	53	51	56	.54***
Masturbates with hand	50***	59	39	.09
Tries to look at people undressing	43	43	44	.00
Touches others' sex parts	33	30	36	-.10
Undresses other people	25	22	28	-.12**
Shows sex parts to adults	21	25	17	.03
Shows sex parts to children	21	24	18	.10
Masturbates with object	16**	12	20	-.06
Looks at nude pictures	16	18	13	.29***
French kissing	15	15	14	-.03
Hugs unfamiliar adults	15	17	13	-.11**
Draws sex parts[2]	13	11	16	.34***
Uses sexual words	11	11	11	.40***
Rubs body against people	10	11	10	-.06
Talks flirtatiously	10	8	12	.05
Talks about sexual acts	8	9	8	.35***
Inserts objects in vagina/anus	4***	1	7	-.03
Makes sexual sounds	4	3	4	-.01
Asks to engage in sex acts	3	3	3	.03
Imitates sexual behavior with dolls	2**	1	4	-.01
Asks to watch explicit tv	1	1	2	.28***

[1]Asterisks indicate significant differences between boys and girls.
[2]Not in scale Friedrich et al. (1991).
* $p < .05$, ** $p < .01$, *** $p < .001$.

older (Table 1). Behaviors which are more frequently observed when the child gets older are: showing interest in the opposite sex, playing doctor, asking questions about sexuality, looking at nude pictures, drawing sexual parts, using sexual words, talking about sexual acts and asking to watch sexually explicit TV. Behaviors that are observed less in older children are: touching mother's breasts, undressing other people, and hugging unfamiliar adults.

There are only a few behaviors that are observed with a different frequency in boys and girls (Table 1). Boys are observed more frequently to touch their own sexual parts and to masturbate using their hands. In girls the following behaviors are more frequently observed by the mothers: playing doctor, masturbating with an object, inserting objects in the vagina or anus, and imitating sexual behaviors with dolls. The latter two behaviors are rather infrequently observed in either boys or girls, though.

The reports of the various sexual behaviors are interrelated: if one specific behavior has been observed, it is likely that another behavior has been observed as well. Together, the items seem to form a reliable scale. Although there is no difference in the mean scale scores of the boys and the girls, there is a small positive correlation with age, indicating that mothers observe more sexual behaviors in older than in younger children (r = .13, p < .001).

There were almost no differences between the mothers regarding the observations of the various sexual behaviors in their children. Although not high, there are two significant correlations. Firstly, it seemed that in families that show higher levels of physical intimacy and are more open towards nudity, mothers observe more sexual behavior in their child (r = .12, p < .01). Secondly, mothers who hold more permissive attitudes towards sexuality also observed higher levels of sexual behavior in their children (r = .18, p < .001). Both characteristics, nature of physical intimacy at home and sexual permissiveness were related as well (r = .26, p > .001).

Behavior that deviates extremely from gender role stereotypes is only rarely reported (Table 2). Differences between boys and girls are in the expected direction: boys more often play with typical boys' toys, while girls do the reverse. The proportion of girls playing with typical boys' toys is however bigger than the proportion of boys playing with typical girls' toys. A preference for gender atypical toys to play with, indicating a desire to be the opposite sex, and pretending

TABLE 2. Observed Gender Atypical Behaviors in Children (0-11 years; percentage endorsement)

Item (abbreviated)	Total[1]	Boys	Girls	r age
Wants to be opposite sex	10	10	10	.02
Pretends to be opposite sex	20	19	21	.05
Plays with typical boy toys	92***	97	88	.01
Plays with typical girl toys	75***	60	92	.01

[1]Asterisks indicate significant differences between boys and girls.
* $p < .05$, ** $p < .01$, *** $p < .001$.

to be the opposite sex are not related to the age of the child, regardless of gender. The mothers do not differ regarding age and level of education regarding the extent to which they report observing atypical gender role behavior. Atypical gender role behavior is related to the tendency to show sexual behavior in general in the sense that children with a higher level of sexual behavior are also reported to display somewhat more cross gender behavior ($r = .19, p < .001$).

DISCUSSION

The findings of this study show that sexual behavior, or what adults usually label as such, is widespread among children and can even be observed in young children. It should be noted, however, that our conclusions are based on observations from a select group of people, i.e., female readers of a Dutch magazine who were willing to take time to fill out a questionnaire. The fact that the level of education of these mothers was relatively high further confirms that we are dealing with a selective group. Furthermore, the findings are based on observations made by the mothers instead of independent observers. Several factors might have influenced the mothers' observations.

One of the factors affecting the mothers' observations is opportunity. The mother needed to be present when the child exhibited the specific behaviors. It might well be that children at a certain age know that they should conceal certain behaviors, in order to prevent negative responses from their parents. There might be other reasons why the child's behavior remains unnoticed.

Another factor limiting the validity of the observations, is the mothers' attitude towards sexuality. It is likely that mothers who hold more permissive sexual attitudes are more open or prepared to observe sexual behavior or label it as such, than restrictive women are willing to do. This is one of the possible explanations for the finding that sexual attitudes are related to level of observed sexual activity in the child. It is, however, impossible to rule out another interpretation, which is that permissive mothers are less discouraging or even encouraging of sexuality in their child than restrictive mothers are. In the latter case, higher levels of sexuality in the child would be much more a consequence of the mother's sexual attitude. More complex interpretations are possible, too. It could be that children of restrictive mothers learn that specific behaviors are not done. Instead of stopping these behaviors they might continue to perform them, albeit secretively. With the data available it is not possible to determine what causes what. Quite likely we are dealing with processes in which various factors affect each other. As a consequence, however, we can not establish the validity of observations of the mothers. This should also be taken into account when we subsequently discuss some other findings.

The relationships between age of the child and some of the sexual behaviors observed can be interpreted in two ways. The decreases of specific behaviors with age can result from incorporating a sense of what is and what is not appreciated or allowed in social interactions. The behaviors that are observed more frequently in older children can be seen as related to the acquisition of specific skills, such as verbal skills, cognitive skills and motor skills. Furthermore, some of these behaviors require at least some understanding of what sexuality is. From a developmental perspective it should have been expected that behaviors, such as asking to watch sexually explicit TV, be observed more frequently in older children. Especially regarding the behaviors that increase with age the correlations are relatively high. These findings stress on the one hand the need to study child sexuality in the context of other developmental processes. On the other hand, child sexuality should be studied in relation to the child-rearing practices of both parents. Studying child sexuality from this broader perspective will help to understand why some children do perform specific behaviors, while others don't.

The finding that older children show more sexual behavior is not in line with what is generally reported. Childhood sexual behavior is supposed to decrease with age, and for girls even more rapidly than for boys. That an opposite trend is observed here is probably partly due to the behaviors that are sampled in the inventory; a selection of childhood sexual behaviors which are more characteristic of young children, would have resulted in an overall decrease in sexual behavior.

The few gender differences are predominantly related to masturbation and can be interpreted to result from anatomical differences between girls and boys. Given these differences, manually masturbating is a more complex skill to learn for a girl than for a boy. At the same time, girls might experience more pleasurable sensations from masturbating with an object than boys do.

The fact that, regardless of the relationships of age and gender with some of the behavioral items, the items form an internally consistent scale is an interesting finding. It suggests that there is a general tendency to show sexually related behaviors, which is more or less strongly present in children. This tendency could be seen as a personality characteristic or a disposition. It could well be that this tendency is a precursor of differential levels of sexual desires in adults.

Although the sexual behavior scale informs us about the omnipresence or rareness of specific behaviors in children, one might debate the validity from a more general perspective, as well as the overall meaning of the scale. Even if one assumes that the observations by the mothers are valid, one might question whether the selected behaviors really tell us something about children's sexuality. A related question is what actually constitutes 'normal' sexual behavior.

A first issue to discuss in this context is what the selected behaviors really tell us about child sexuality. From the outside, these behaviors seem to be clearly sexual. It should be acknowledged, however, that these behaviors get a sexual meaning in the perception of the adult observers (cf. Plummer, 1991). It is unclear how the children themselves experience these behaviors. Some children, especially the older ones, might be aware that because of their parents' responses these behaviors have an exceptional meaning to adults. It is likely, though, that only few children will experience or perceive these behaviors as sexual. To be able to do so, they at least need to have a sense of what sexuality is. For a full understanding of child sexuality, one should also try to explore the meaning specific behaviors have for children themselves (see Rademakers et al., this volume). It is likely that as soon as the child is aware of the label of sexuality and the cultural connotations attached to it, it will affect the behavior itself as well as the way in which that behavior is experienced. This will happen regardless of whether the child has a full understanding of the concept.

The lack of correspondence between the meaning attached to the behavior by parent and child will affect the interaction between the parent and the child. By labeling the child's behaviors as sexual, the parents single out a particular set of behaviors and give it a specific symbolic meaning. By labeling these behaviors as sexual, parents might also attribute motivations to the child's behavior that are not necessarily present. This attribution of meaning to the child's behavior will affect the way parents respond to the child when he or she exhibits these behaviors. The child may not always understand why their behavior is responded to so exceptionally.

A second issue is whether or not the scale informs us about what is normal sexual behavior in children. Knowing that a specific behavior is exhibited by a large group of same-aged children might comfort parents who worry about their child's behavior. But what to tell to parents when their child performs acts that are rarely observed? It should be realized that the sexual behavior scale originally was developed as an instrument to assess whether a child has had sexually abusive experiences. Some of the items on the scale result from discussions Friedrich and his co-workers had with parents of sexually abused children (Friedrich et al., 1991). He has shown that the scale indeed is able to differentiate quite successfully between sexually abused and non-abused children; the abused children having higher mean scores on the scale. This higher score did not turn out to be the result of higher ratings on some specific items, but from higher ratings in general. This higher score is interpreted as the empirical validation of Finkelhor's traumagenic factor of sexualization (Finkelhor, 1986). It is unclear whether the child is really more sexually active compared to his age mates, or whether the mother, because of the child's experiences, is more perceptive of the child's behavior. It could well be that specific behaviors are now seen as sexual, while before the abuse they were not recognized or labeled as such. Regardless of this issue, the question remains how middle and low scores on the scale should be interpreted. What are these scores indicative of? Should one be concerned if a child shows too low levels of sexual behavior as measured by this scale? What should be seen as a normal level of sexual activity, if there is such a thing? How much normal variation is there between children? Is there a relationship between levels of sexual behavior in siblings of the same family? Do reports of fathers and mothers differ?

Further research in this field would profit from a more explicit conceptualization of what child sexuality is. To get a better understanding of what motivates specific behaviors, different kinds of data have to be incorporated in the study as well. The findings from this study furthermore suggest that in order to understand child sexuality, other developmental dimensions as well as the cultural milieu in which the child develops should also be taken into account. If we assume that child sexual experiences affect later sexual functioning, this topic deserves to be studied more extensively, and not just in the context of abuse.

REFERENCES

Finkelhor, D. (Ed.) (1986). *A Sourcebook on Child Sexual Abuse*. Beverly Hills: Sage.

Friedrich, W.N., Grambsch, P., Broughton, D., Kuiper B.S., & Beilke, R.L. (1991). Normative sexual behavior in children. *Pediatrics*, 88: 456-464.

Plummer, K. (1990). Understanding childhood sexualities. In Sandfort, T.G.M., Brongersma, E., & Van Naerssen, A. (Eds.), *Male Intergenerational Intimacy: Historical, Socio-psychological, and Legal Perspectives* (pp. 231-249). New York: The Haworth Press, Inc.

Van Zessen, G., & Sandfort, T.G.M. (1991). *Seksualiteit in Nederland. Seksueel gedrag, risico en preventie van AIDS*. Amsterdam: Swets & Zeitlinger.

Cultural Differences in Sexual Behavior: 2-6 Year Old Dutch and American Children

William N. Friedrich, PhD
Theo G. M. Sandfort, PhD
Jacqueline Oostveen, MD
Peggy T. Cohen-Kettenis, PhD

ABSTRACT. Three samples, one American (N = 500) and two from the Netherlands (N = 460, N = 297) of 2-6 year old children, screened for the absence of sexual abuse, were assessed with 25 items derived from the Child Sexual Behavior Inventory (Friedrich et al. 1992). Considerable differences existed between the three groups across a number of the behaviors rated, with a persisting tendency for the parents of the children from the Netherlands to report higher rates of sexual behavior. Family nudity was related to sexual behavior in all three samples. Although the studies used an equivalent questionnaire and all three of the samples are predominantly middle class, the observed differences can be explained by methodological factors such as sample composition and the way data have been collected. The observed differences might, however, also reflect actual differences, and can be understood as resulting from cultural differences in sexual socialization. More rigorous research is needed to assess which explanation is most valid. *[Article copies available for a fee from The Haworth Document Delivery Service: 1-800-342-9678. E-mail address: <getinfo@haworthpressinc.com> Website: <http://www.HaworthPress. com>]*

William N. Friedrich is affiliated with Mayo Clinic, Rochester, MN. Theo G. M. Sandfort and Peggy T. Cohen-Kettenis are affiliated with Utrecht University, The Netherlands. Jacqueline Oostveen is affiliated with General Health Service, Hilversum, The Netherlands.

[Haworth co-indexing entry note]: "Cultural Differences in Sexual Behavior: 2-6 Year Old Dutch and American Children." Friedrich, William N. et al. Co-published simultaneously in *Journal of Psychology & Human Sexuality* (The Haworth Press, Inc.) Vol. 12, No. 1/2, 2000, pp. 117-129; and: *Childhood Sexuality: Normal Sexual Behavior and Development* (ed: Theo G. M. Sandfort, and Jany Rademakers) The Haworth Press, Inc., 2000, pp. 117-129. Single or multiple copies of this article are available for a fee from The Haworth Document Delivery Service [1-800-342-9678, 9:00 a.m. - 5:00 p.m. (EST). E-mail address: getinfo@haworth pressinc.com].

KEYWORDS. Child Sexual Behavior Inventory, parents' observations, cross-cultural differences, family nudity

The sexual behavior of young children has generated considerably more interest of late, particularly with the persistent finding about the relationship between sexual abuse and sexual behavior (Friedrich, 1993). This finding has resulted in greater confusion, by parents and clinicians, about what constitutes normal sexual behavior in children. Clinicians and educators are asked more frequent questions about the normalcy of one behavior or another, and there are few definitive resources (Martinson, 1976).

This paper is based on two premises. The first premise is that sexual behavior in children is normal, expected, and includes a broad range of behaviors (Friedrich, Grambsch, Broughton, Kuiper, & Beilke, 1991). The second premise is that it is absolutely important to examine sexual behavior in context, not isolation.

Several recent studies, using large community-based samples, and relying on parent report, have established the normalcy of sexual behavior in children. For example, one study by Rosenfeld and colleagues (Rosenfeld, Bailey, Siegel, and Bailey, 1986), with a sample of 576 children aged 2-10, found that children touching parents' breasts or genitals was not uncommon on an incidental basis.

In another study, Friedrich and colleagues (Friedrich et al., 1991) screened 880 children, ages 2-12, across 36 sexual behaviors with the Child Sexual Behavior Inventory (CSBI). They found that in this sample, screened for the absence of sexual abuse, that even behaviors thought to be unusual, were reported at some level of frequency, e.g., mouth on sex parts, masturbates with object, inserts objects in vagina or rectum. The conclusion from earlier writing and these empirical studies is clear–sexual behavior can be expected in normal children.

The second premise, the role of context, has also been studied. Friedrich et al. (1991) found that family nudity was directly related to the report of sexual behavior in normal children. In another study, he and his colleagues found that both life stress and sexual abuse were also directly related to sexual behavior; the majority of the sexual behaviors studied were reported with significantly greater incidence in sexually abused children (Friedrich, Grambsch Damon, Hewitt, Koverola, Lang, Wolfe, & Broughton, 1992).

Another very important context is cultural. We know from cross-cultural studies that sexual behavior varies from culture to culture (Martinson, 1976; Rutter, 1991; Hofstede, 1998; Hubert, Bajos & Sandfort, 1998). Behavior related to sexual activity, i.e., teenage pregnancy, also varies from one country to the next. For example, a 37-country analysis found teenage birth rate to be inversely related to liberal sexual views and equitable distribution of income. In a more detailed, six-country analysis, i.e., U.S., England, France, Canada, Sweden, and the Netherlands, the U.S. had the highest rate of teenage pregnancy across all age levels and had reduced use of contraceptives despite relatively high rates of sexual activity (Jones, Forrest, Goldman, Henshaw, Lincoln, Rosoff, Westoff, and Wulf, 1985). The Netherlands had the lowest rate of these six countries. The authors commented that "In the United States, sex tends to be treated as a special topic, and there is much ambivalence . . . romantic but also sinful . . . flaunted but also something to be hidden" (p. 59).

We were given a unique opportunity to examine cultural differences in sexual behavior in young children in the United States and the Netherlands. Both of these countries share a Western culture and are similar on three of four emperically based major, independent dimensions of national cultures: Power Distance (unequal versus equal), Individualism/Collectivism (alone versus together) and Uncertainty Avoidance (rigid versus flexible) (Hofstede, 1991). They differ, though, substantively on the fourth dimension: Masculinity/Femininity (tough versus tender), the United States being a more masculine and the Netherlands being a more feminine society. Masculine and feminine societies differ with respect to general values, relationships between men and women, child rearing practices, the organization of work, as well as national policies. Masculine and feminine societies also differ regarding sexuality, the latter generally being more permissive (Hofstede, 1998). That the Netherlands has a more permissive sexual climate than the United States has also been documented in the World Values Studies (Van den Akker, Halman & De Moor, 1994).

A briefer version of the CSBI used in the Friedrich et al. (1991, 1992) studies was administered to two large samples of parents of 2-6 year old Dutch children. This allowed a comparison about reported rates of sexual behavior in two different countries.

METHOD

U. S. Sample

The 2-6 year old children reported in this study are from the 880 non-abused, 2-12 year old children described in Friedrich et al. (1991). Subjects were recruited from families who used a primary care pediatric clinic. Eligible families had at least one child between 2 and 12 years of age, had resided in North America for at least three years, and resided in one of the eight immediately surrounding counties normally served by this clinic. Only mothers were used as reporters, and they were recruited in the clinic waiting room by a trained female research assistant who used a random sampling design for recruitment. Natural or adoptive mothers accounted for 99.6 percent of the mothers; the remainder, stepmothers. After signing an Informed Consent, the mother completed a questionnaire about her child.

Of 1,231 eligible families, 871 returned questionnaires for a rate of 70.8 percent. From a total of 1,091 completed surveys, 211 surveys were eliminated from the analyses for one or more reasons, including living outside of the eight county primary catchment area of the clinic, the child had a chronic physical or mental condition, the child had received counseling in the past, or the child had a confirmed or suspected history of sexual abuse. Other questionnaires were excluded for having excessive blank answers. This resulted in a final and total sample of 880 children, of whom 500 were 2-6 years of age. The total sample represented 80.6 percent of those who initially returned surveys.

For each sample, the mother was asked to rate the frequency of behavior in the past 6 months. Frequency ranged from "never," to "less than once per month," to "1-3 times per month," to "at least once per week." Tables 1 and 2 present the demographic data and age and sex distributions for the sample.

Dutch Magazine Sample (DMS)

A questionnaire was developed that included a broad-based assessment of general behavior in children, gender role, sexual knowledge, nudity in the home, the parents' previous sexual experiences–including sexual abuse, and background information regarding the child's age, education level of the parents, and living arrangements. In addition, 25 items from the Child Sexual Behavior Inventory were translated into Dutch by two of the authors (TS, PTC-K) and included in the questionnaire. To insure the accuracy of the translation, the questionnaire was back-translated into English. Almost all items turned out to have an exact identical meaning. A few items differed, resulting in somewhat higher endorsement thresholds either for the U.S. sample or for the Dutch sample. It is very unlikely, though, that these differences are the cause of the observed systematic differences.

The questionnaire was included in the editorial page of the September, 1990, issue of the Dutch magazine, *Ouders van nu* (*Parents Today*), which is a magazine intended for young parents. It averages 180,000 subscriptions per year. The readership is primarily 25-35 year old females who tend to live in the smaller cities and towns of the Netherlands. Although 716 completed questionnaires were returned (< 1% of the subscription base) only data provided by mothers of 2-6 year old children was utilized (N = 460). Questionnaires completed by fathers (N = 55), or for 7-11 year olds (N = 143) were not included, as well as questionnaires not completely filled out (N = 58).

Dutch Health Service Sample (DHS)

The identical questionnaire used in *Ouders van nu* (*Parents Today*) was administered to the parents of healthy children who presented for regular physical checkups to a school doctor with the Municipal Health Service. None of the parents had completed the questionnaire earlier and the refusal rate was 27.8 percent. A total of 372 questionnaires were obtained. Only those completed by mothers on 2-6 year old children (N = 297) were utilized. The remaining questionnaires were completed either on older children or by fathers.

All three groups of observed children come from educated, middle-class families with an average of two children. All three samples were specifically screened regarding possible or actual sexual abuse. Differences include the fact that the Dutch magazine sample averages .72

TABLE 1. Demographic Data on Three Samples

Variables	American	Dutch Magazine	Dutch Health Service
Child's Age	4.2	3.5	5.4
% Female	50.4	48.5	47.8

TABLE 2. Age and Sex Distribution of Samples

	Age in Years					Totals
	2	3	4	5	6	
U.S. Male	12	71	50	60	55	248
Dutch Mag. Male	59	74	52	29	23	237
Dutch Hlth. Svc. Male	0	0	3	98	54	155
U.S. Female	21	66	62	56	47	252
Dutch Mag. Female	55	69	50	25	24	223
Dutch Hlth Svc. Female	0	1	3	87	51	142

years younger than the U.S. sample, and the Dutch Health Service sample averaged approximately one year older than the U.S. sample. An examination of Table 2, which lists the age distribution, reveals that significantly more of the 2 year olds were from the Dutch magazine sample. The sample from the Dutch Health Service, where children are seen who attend school, was generally in the 4-6 year range. Please refer to Tables 1 and 2 for demographic information.

RESULTS

Because of the different methods of data collection utilized for each sample, we chose to examine qualitative differences between the three groups. For example, we examined those behaviors in which the endorsement frequency, i.e., present, not present, differed between the groups by more than 5 percentage points.

For the females, 20 of the 25 behaviors differed by more than 5 percentage points, and in almost all cases, the behaviors were seen more frequently in either one or both of the Dutch samples (Table 3). They included the following: asks to engage in sex acts, masturbates with object, inserts objects in vagina, sexual sounds, French kisses, undresses other people, imitates sexual behavior with dolls, wants to be the opposite sex, talks about sexual acts, touches other people's sex parts, shows sex parts to children, uses sexual words, talks flirtatiously, masturbates with hand, looks at nude pictures, interested in the opposite sex, tries to look at people when undressing, touches breasts of others, touches sex parts at home, and gender differences with regards to toy preference. In addition, 14 of these 20 behaviors were reported significantly more often by both Dutch groups, i.e., at least 20 percentage point difference.

TABLE 3. Dutch/U.S. Female Endorsement Contrasts

No a.	Item (abbreviated)	Dutch Mag. Girls 2-6 (N = 223)	Dutch Hlth. Sv. Girls 3-6 (N = 142)	U.S. Girls 2-6 (N = 252)
15.	Asks to engage in sex acts	2.7	6.3	0.0
7.	Masturbates with object	20.2	14.7	0.8
17.	Inserts objects in vagina/anus	7.2	9.1	2.8
14.	Sexual sounds	4.0	7.7	0.8
30.	French kisses	12.6	17.5	4.0
28.	Undresses other people	28.3	21.0	4.4
29.	Asks to watch explicit TV	0.0	6.3	1.6
19.	Imitates sexual behavior with dolls	2.7	7.7	0.8
2.	Wants to be opposite sex	11.2	14.7	7.5
22.	Talks about sexual acts	4.5	12.6	2.8
8.	Touches other's sex parts	37.7	32.9	5.6
16.	Rubs body against people	8.5	7.0	8.3
31.	Hugs strange adults	11.7	11.2	14.3
32.	Shows sex parts to children	16.1	21.0	7.5
12.	Uses sexual words	6.7	19.6	1.2
27.	Talks flirtatiously	10.8	25.9	15.9
13.	Pretends to be opposite sex	21.1	21.7	20.6
4.	Masturbates with hand	36.8	35.7	16.3
21.	Looks at nude pictures	8.5	18.2	7.9
20.	Shows sex parts to adults	14.8	16.1	17.9
34.	Interested in opposite sex	63.7	66.5	20.6
18.	Tries to look at people undressing	43.9	44.8	33.3
6.	Touches breasts	80.3	78.3	48.4
11.	Touches sex parts at home	96.0	84.6	54.4
35.	Boy-girl toys	87.4	78.3	71.4

aNo. corresponds to the CSBI Item Number reported in Friedrich et al. (1991).

For the males, using the same 5 percentage point discrepancy, differences existed on 22 of the 25 behaviors, with overlap on 19 of the 20 behaviors shown more often by the Dutch females (Table 4). Boys did not show the same frequency of preference for female toys as shown by girls for male toys. In addition, 11 of these 22 behaviors were shared by both Dutch male samples. Both samples of Dutch males were also reported to hug strange adults significantly more often than American males.

The Dutch groups were not identical, however. The Dutch Health Service sample (DHS) contributed 8 additional differences over the 12 that the DHS and the Dutch Magazine sample (DMS) shared for the females. The male DHS contributed 11 additional differences over the 11 the DHS and DMS shared.

It is possible that some of the additional differences reported in the

TABLE 4. Dutch/U.S. Male Endorsement Contrasts

No.[a] Item (abbreviated)	Dutch Mag. Boys 2-6 (N = 237)	Dutch Hlth. Sv. Boys 4-6 (N = 155)	U.S. Boys 2-6 (N = 248)
15. Asks to engage in sex acts	2.1	8.1	1.2
7. Masturbates with object	11.8	12.7	0.8
17. Inserts objects in vagina/anus	1.3	8.1	0.0
14. Sexual sounds	2.5	9.4	0.4
30. French kisses	16.5	15.7	1.6
28. Undresses other people	18.6	18.9	4.4
29. Asks to watch explicit TV	0.4	7.5	0.0
19. Imitates sexual behavior with dolls	0.8	8.8	0.8
2. Wants to be opposite sex	9.7	15.1	7.3
22. Talks about sexual acts	5.1	12.5	2.4
8. Touches other's sex parts	28.7	23.3	8.9
16. Rubs body against people	11.4	10.0	8.5
31. Hugs strange adults	19.4	13.2	6.5
32. Shows sex parts to children	23.6	29.5	15.7
12. Uses sexual words	6.3	27.7	4.8
27. Talks flirtatiously	8.4	14.4	8.5
13. Pretends to be opposite sex	20.3	20.1	16.9
4. Masturbates with hand	57.4	45.3	22.6
21. Looks at nude pictures	14.3	23.3	11.3
20. Shows sex parts to adults	26.6	30.8	25.8
34. Interested in opposite sex	64.1	54.0	21.0
18. Tries to look at people undressing	43.9	40.2	33.9
6. Touches breasts	73.8	59.7	43.5
11. Touches sex parts at home	96.6	91.8	64.1
35. Boy-girl toys	56.6	54.7	63.3

[a]No. corresponds to the CSBI Item Number reported in Friedrich et al. (1991).

DHS sample are due to the relatively older age of this sample. Although age trends were not noted in the DMS sample, sexual behavior was higher in the 4-5 year old children in the U.S. sample than in the 2-3 year olds.

The largest differences between the U.S. sample and either one or both Dutch samples, i.e., by 20 percentage points or more, occur for a total of 7 female behaviors and 5 male behaviors, with 4 overlapping items. For both boys and girls these behaviors include: touching one's genitals at home (Item No. 11), touching breasts (Item No. 6), masterbates with hand (Item No. 4), and showing interest in the opposite sex (Item No. 34).

Interestingly, the established differences in reported behaviors between boys and girls are generally consistent across the two countries (again applying the 5 percent criterion). In both countries more boys than girls are reported to show sex parts to other children and to adults (Items No. 32 and 20), to touch their sex parts at home (Item No. 11) and to masturbate using their hand (Item No. 4). Girls in both countries are reported more often to talk flirtatiously (Item No. 27) and to exhibit cross-gender toy selection (Item No. 35). With respect to hugging strange adults (Item No. 31) the differences are opposite: While more Dutch boys are reported by their mothers to do so, American parents report this behavior more frequently about their daughters. Next to the behaviors mentioned, there are more gender differences in the reports of the Dutch parents, although not completely consistent for both samples. For American parents there are no further gender differences.

Further analyses focused on the influence of certain behaviors related to family sexuality on the presence of sexual behavior in these children. As reported in Friedrich et al. (1991), family nudity was positively correlated with overall frequency of reported sexual behavior in children, i.e., total score on the CSBI. Family nudity was reflected in a family sexuality index which was the sum of the following variables: nude pictures available in the home, bathes with adults, sees nude adults in home, witnessed intercourse, and sees nudity on television. For the U.S. sample, the correlation of total CSBI and the family sexuality index was significant ($r = .18$, $p < .04$).

A related index was created for both Dutch samples using behaviors rated by the parents. They included parental nudity, bathing with children, and a rating of parent permissiveness. The total score was correlated with the sum of the 25 items of the checklist. There was a significant relationship between the family sexuality index and reported sexual behavior in children for both Dutch samples as well. The correlation for the DMS was $r = .20$, $p = .02$ and for DHS, $r = .21$, $p = .03$. Taken together, these correlations suggest that the context variable of family sexuality is related to the reported frequency of sexual behavior in children.

DISCUSSION

The findings from this study can be interpreted in two ways, one reflecting similarities and the other differences between the American and the Dutch samples. Approximately one half of the rated behaviors

(13 of 25 for the females and 13 of 25 for the males) were within 5 percentage points for the U.S. sample and at least one of the two Dutch samples, typically the Dutch magazine sample. This would suggest the relative similarity between these samples. Behaviors that are relatively unusual among the American children, e.g., inserts objects in vagina or rectum, asks to engage in sex acts, for the most part are relatively unusual in the Dutch children. The fact that family sexual behavior was related to child sexual behavior in the Dutch samples and in the American sample and that gender differences in reported behavior were generally consistent, add to the commonalties among the three samples.

Another way to examine this data would be to emphasize the differences between the two countries, with 20 or 22 of 25 of the behaviors, depending upon the gender, differing by more than 5 percentage points for at least one of the Dutch samples. For example, the item pertaining to French kissing, or "inserts tongue in other person's mouth when kissing," is far more common in the Dutch sample. However, only 5 or 7 of these 25 behaviors, again dependent upon gender, differ by a very large amount, i.e., 20 percent or greater.

The observed differences between the American and the Dutch samples can be interpreted in various ways. First of all, the differences could result from methodological characteristics of the three studies. There are clear differences in the way in which the sample for each study was obtained. The families in the DHS had a relationship with the school doctor based on trust. As a consequence, they may have responded more openly than the two groups where mothers reported anonymously. However, the differences between the DHS and the DMS samples are not systematic: sometimes mothers in one sample report more sexual behavior of their child, with respect to other sexual behaviors mothers in the other sample do so. With regard to the DMS sample, which constituted less than one percent of the magazine's subscription base, it is quite likely that selection of respondents affected the reports. Presumably more conservative parents, if ever they were subscribers to that magazine, would choose not to respond. Another methodological factor explaining the observed differences might be the wording of the questionnaire. Although backward translation resulted in a satisfactory equivalence, some of the items might have been perceived differently by the Dutch-speaking mothers.

The last consistent difference between the groups was age, with the samples ranging from an average of 3.5 years to 5.4 years. However, the relation with age was not linear across the three samples, as the U.S. sample averaged 4.2 years old. It is expected that age is not the primary factor for the differences reported.

Another methodological factor might be the differential reliability of the mothers' reports. Some of the observed differences are in regard to behaviors which are quite common, such as "touching sex parts while at home" (Item No. 11) and "showing interest in the opposite sex" (Item No. 34). It would be unusual for a 2-6 year old child not to touch their genitals, at least once, in the preceding six months. It is also likely that many 2-6 year old children, when being fed or held, touch their mother's breasts. With respect to these behaviors, the Dutch mothers may have reported frequencies that are closer to actuality, while American mothers failed to observe the quite natural and common sexual behaviors of a child.

These differences in the reliability of the observations might be related to parents' attitudes toward sexuality in general and child sexuality in particular. It has been shown in this respect that the attitudes of people in the Netherlands, as a more feminine society, are more permissive than those of the people in the United States (Hofstede, 1998; Van den Akker et al., 1994). Some of the observed higher frequencies of sexual behavior as reported by Dutch mothers might be a result of more permissive attitudes. This interpretation is supported by recent data with a new version of the CSBI, showing that parent attitude about child sexuality is significantly related to the parents' report of sexual behavior (Friedrich, Fisher, Broughton, Houston, & Shafran, 1998). Those parents who do not believe child sexuality is normal report fewer sexual behaviors in their child.

Although methodological factors might explain the observed differences, it is also possible that the observed differences reflect real differences and that Dutch children are somewhat more overtly sexual than their American counterparts. Since it is unlikely that Dutch children are more sexual than American children by nature, these differences would then be a consequence of early sexual and bodily socialization. Since Dutch and American attitudes towards sexuality differ, it is quite likely that their related child rearing practices vary as well. Relative to Dutch parents, American parents may have a less positive attitude, and if so, they may negatively reinforce specific behaviors. As a consequence, these behaviors might either disappear or only be expressed in the absence of the parents. This interpretation is not conflicting with the just reported finding of Friedrich et al. (1998). Parents who do not believe child sexuality is normal report fewer sexual behaviors in their child, and this may be a consequence of more restrictive sexual socialization. A parallel reasoning can be developed regarding the finding that family nudity was positively correlated with overall frequency of reported sexual behavior in children.

As indicated, the data need to be interpreted with some caution for various reasons. The results of this study do, however, affirm both premises presented in the introduction. Sexual behavior occurs in children who are described as normal, and a national cultural as well as familial context is important to consider in determining on a statistical level what is normal and what is not. Future research is currently under way in which samples obtained via a very similar recruitment method are contrasted empirically (Schoentjes, Leeman, Pastijn, Deboutte, & Friedrich, in preparation). This will be a truer test of the differences noted. In order to understand possible differences, such studies should include people's attitudes toward sexuality, sexual education practices, as well as the way in which parents deal with the child's body and its bodily functions.

REFERENCES

Friedrich, W.N. (1993). Sexual victimization and sexual behavior in children: A review of recent literature. *Child Abuse and Neglect, 17,* 59-66.

Friedrich, W.N., Fisher, J., Broughton, D., Houston, M., & Shafran, C. (1998). Normative sexual behavior in children: A contemporary sample. *Pediatrics, 101*(4), 9.

Friedrich, W.N., Grambsch, P., Broughton, D., Kuiper, J., & Beilke, R.L. (1991). Normative sexual behavior in children. *Pediatrics, 88,* 456-464.

Friedrich, W.N., Grambsch, P., Damon, L., Hewitt, S.K., Koverola, C., Lang, R.A., Wolfe, V., & Broughton, D. (1992). Child Sexual Behavior Inventory: Normative and clinical comparisons. *Psychological Assessment, 4,* 303-311.

Hofstede, G. (1991). *Cultures and organizations: Software of the mind.* London: McGraw-Hill.

Hofstede, G. (1998). Comparative studies of sexual behavior: Sex as achievement or as relationship? In G. Hofstede (Ed.). *Masculinity and feminity. The taboo dimension of national cultures* (pp. 153-178). Thousand Oaks, CA: Sage.

Hubert, M., Bajos, N., & Sandfort, T. (1998). *Sexual behaviour and HIV/AIDS in Europe.* London: UCL Press.

Jones, E.F., Forrest, J.D., Goldman, N., Henshaw, S.K., Lincoln, R., Rosoff, J.I., Westoff, C.F., and Wulf, D. (1985). Teenage pregnancy in developed countries: Determinants and policy implications. *Family Planning Perspectives, 17* (2), 53-63.

Martinson, F.M. (1976). Eroticism in infancy and childhood. *Journal of Sex Research, 12*, 251-262.

Rosenfeld, A.A., Bailey, R., Siegel, B., and Bailey, G. (1986). Determining incestuous contact between parent and child: Frequency of children touching parents' genitals in a nonclinical population. *Journal of the American Academy of Child Psychiatry, 25*, 481-484.

Rosenfeld, A.A., Siegel-Gorelick, B., Haavik, D., Duryea, M., Wenegrat, A., Martin, J., and Bailey, R. (1984). Parental perceptions of children's modesty: A cross-sectional survey of ages 2-10 years. *Journal of Psychiatry, 47*, 351-365.

Rutter, M. (1991). Normal psychosexual development. *Journal of Child Psychology and Psychiatry*, 259-283.

Schoentjes, E., Leeman, I., Pastijn, I., Deboutte, D., & Friedrich, W. (In preparation). Sexual behavior in children: Using the Child Sexual Behavior Inventory to describe a Dutch-speaking normative sample.

Van den Akker, P., Halman, L., & de Moor, R. (1994). Primary relations in Western societies. In P. Ester, L. Halman, & R. de Moor (eds.), *The individualizing society. Value change in Europe and North America* (pp. 97-127). Tilburg: Tilburg University Press.

Index

Adolescents
pregnancy rate in, 119
sexual behavior/conduct
disorder-related behavior
association in, 63-65
sexually-transmitted disease risk of,
64-65
Age factors, in childhood sexual
behavior, 109-110,112-113.
See also Preschool-aged
children
AIDS. *See also* HIV (human
immunodeficiency virus)
infection
boys' awareness of and attitudes
toward, 86,91,93-94
Animals, cuddling with, 53
Asexuality, of children, 83

Bathing, genital exploration during
with parents, 30,37,41
with siblings, 42
Being in love
children's attitudes toward, 54,55
children's experiences of,
53-54,55,58
parental reports of, 56,57
Birth, children's knowledge of, 31
of preschool children, 6,9,15-17,
18,21-22,23
of school-age children, 22
Birth rate, adolescent, cross-national
differences in, 119
Body awareness, 50
Body care, 36,37-38
Body discovery. *See also* Genital
exploration
process of, 28,29
Body parts. *See also* Genitals

"pleasant and exciting," 29,54-55
Body representation, 28-29
Boys
cross-gender behavior in, 70,
75,122,123,124,125
desire to be girls, 70,110-111
mutual masturbation among, 31
sex interviews with, 84-101
AIDS and sexuality protocol of,
85-86,88,89,91
boys' level of cooperation in, 97
boys' negative attitudes toward,
84,92-94,95,96-97,98
boys' positive attitudes toward,
84,91,96-97
boys' reticence in, 89-90,98-100
boys' sexual vocabulary in,
89-90,98,99
boys' willingness/unwillingness
to participate in, 84,95,96
interview process, 89-90
mothers' negative attitudes
toward, 93,94-95,97
mothers' positive attitudes
toward, 91-92
reliability ratings of, 96-97
as source of worry, 84,93-95,96

Castration anxiety, 30-31
CBCL. *See* Child Behavior Checklist
Cesarean section, preschool children's
knowledge of, 15-16,21
Child Behavior Checklist (CBCL),
65,87
Sex Problems scale, association
with other CBCL scales,
69-75
Childhood sexual behavior
age-related changes in,
109-110,112-113